D1134379

THE
BRIGADIER
DOWN
UNDER

THE BRIGADIER DOWN UNDER

Peter Tinniswood

MACMILLAN LONDON

For Doug Insole of Essex and England,
who became such a good friend to us.
And to Bob Willis and his team,
whom I admire enormously.

Copyright © Peter Tinniswood 1983

Illustrations by John Lawrence

All rights reserved. No part of this publication
may be reproduced or transmitted, in any form
or by any means, without permission.

ISBN 0 333 36293 4

First published 1983 by
Macmillan London Limited
London and Basingstoke

Associated companies in Auckland, Dallas,
Delhi, Dublin, Hong Kong, Johannesburg,
Lagos, Manzini, Melbourne, Nairobi,
New York, Singapore, Tokyo, Washington
and Zaria

Phototypeset by Wyvern Typesetting Limited, Bristol
Printed in Hong Kong

Contents

ONE

The Explanation

I did not want to go there in the first place.

Who in his right mind would?

Australia!

No one word has the power to strike such misery, doom and despondency deep into the vitals of civilized man.

Australia!

Land of ravaged desert, shark-infested ocean and thirst-lashed outback.

Australia!

Land of strange, exotic creatures, freaks of evolution, ghastly victims of Mother Nature's vicious whimsy – kangaroo and platypus, potoroo and bandicoot, Richie Benaud and . . .

Richie Benaud!

No two words have the power to strike such misery, doom and despondency deep into the vitals of civilized man.

I am not a prejudiced man, but . . .

TWO

The Landfall

Well, we have arrived Down Under, the lady wife and I.

Oh, woe is me.

Oh, misery beyond redemption.

Oh, wretchedness beyond compare.

Dear, dear Witney Scrotum – how my heart yearns for you wrapped now in the raiments of English winter, cold mists coiling round the massive summit of Botham's Gut, wild geese wailing in the frost-chapped water meadows at Cowdrey's Bottom and icy dewdrops clanking from the tip of old Granny Swanton's ancient nose.

Ah, the pain of exile!

Ah, the cruelties inflicted on a sensitive soul from noble Albion by this godforsaken hell-hole of a country with its weak, tepid beer, foul Antarctic gales, ugly women with hairy chests and fat bottoms and sun-addled men with no lead in their pencils.

Vileness surrounds on all sides.

Every prospect displeases.

The ghastly sun beats down out of a relentlessly blue and cloudless sky.

Our nostrils are most brutally assaulted by the scents of stale meat pies and fetid armpits.

All we hear is the drone of mosquito, the flip and flop of shuffling feet, the screech of cockatoo, the rattle of beer can, the long-drawn, snivelling winge and whine of the Australian native tongue, and, most vile of all, the cricket commentaries of Richie Benaud.

So why are we here?

Well may you ask, dear readers, well may you ask.

There is only one person on the face of this earth who could have reduced me to such depths of misery and despair.

Of course, dear readers, of course – it is the lady wife.

And why has she dragged me here?

Is it punishment for some dire sin I committed during the summer long since gone?

Did I forget to pull the chain in the ablutions offices "during company?"

Did I knock my pipe out in the goldfish bowl "once too often?"

Did I commit an "error of judgement" by wearing ginger plus fours in the presence of the Pope on the occasion of the Holy Father's personal pilgrimage to Witney Scrotum to pay homage to the tomb of the unknown leg spinner?

No.

The answer is more hideous by far.

We are here Down Under in order to visit the lady wife's unmarried spinster brother, Naunton.

Dear God, in my innocence I had thought I was forever free of his rampant loathsomeness when the beast was banished from the Mother Country following "an incident" in his regiment involving a trench mortar, half a bar of nougat and a well-known Wiltshire occasional seamer.

This, however, was not the case.

During the late summer, to my profound distress, the lady wife received intelligence that the vileness was "alive and kicking" in some Australian out-back town, the name of which, as is the case with most other towns in this godforsaken country, sounds like some highly-contagious disease of the private parts.

Apparently he was "earning his crust" selling marsupial underpants to incontinent wicket keepers and bringing succour and comfort to lonely cricketers through the medium of life-sized, inflatable rubber dolls in the shape of Messrs Rodney Marsh and Dennis Lillee.

The lady wife, with the typical impetuosity of her gender, which is female, had to see him at once.

In vain did I plead for mercy.

If we were away for winter, who, I said, would feed and water old Granny Swanton, who would man the hot Bovril kiosk at the golf ball museum, who would run the Christmas raffle for defrocked umpires at the Baxter Arms?

The lady wife was adamant.

She fixed me with those pink and piggy little eyes of hers and boomed in those familiar hectoring tones:

"I don't know what you're making such a fuss about. You can watch the cricket, can't you?"

Watch the cricket?

Watch the cricket, did she say?

Good God, one doesn't watch cricket in Australia.

One listens to it.

On the talking wireless.

In the depths of an English winter.

At the crack of cold, grey dawn.

In the Commodore's summer house, wrapped in Vick-impregnated I Zingari mufflers and fortified by flasks of Instant Possum and whisky-flavoured cream crackers.

One sits "glued" to the talking wireless, preening with pleasure, crooning with delight, as "over the ether" ring the sweet and dulcet tones of Lord Henry Blofeld, the profound and majestic sermons of Cardinal Bailey and the sharp, barked commands of the leader of the BBC Blackshirt Brigade, Don "Sir Oswald" Mosey.

But of these matters, I fear, the "opposite gender"

is ignorant, every man jack of them.

Scum!

What do they know of the "finer things of life?"

Have they ever worn spats?

No.

Have they ever driven a snorting, snarling steam locomotive up Lickey Bank or gone twelve rounds with Randolph Turpin?

No.

Have they ever edited Wisden's Almanack, smelled the inside of Mr Ian Botham's socks, kissed the chaste and pure Mr David Gower, sandpapered the toenails of an Airedale terrier, held the post of Prime Minister of the United Kingdom?

Of course not.

I am not a prejudiced man, but, if I had my way, I should . . .

No matter.

No matter, dear readers.

Suffice it to say that on a dour and sullen November morn we set forth for Australia.

Farewell Witney Scrotum.

The villagers lined the streets wailing and wringing their hands.

The church bells tolled.

The sightscreens on the village green were blackened and turned inwards and the flag flew at half mast on the roof of Squire Brearley's Indoor Knitting School.

Outside the Baxter Arms poor old doddery Arlott shuffled forwards and touched his grizzled forelock.

"Promise me one thing, sir," he said. "Don't touch the Aussie claret. If you wants a good tipple, sir, take my advice and only drink the Château Trumper Spaetauslese, 1967. He be a noble drink, sir. A noble drink."

I slipped the poor wretch a 20p Peter Dominic gift voucher, and he seemed well-pleased.

The Commodore insisted on driving us to the rail-head, from which we were to embark for London.

He wept copiously throughout the journey, and at the station buildings he gripped my hand firmly and said:

"Shall I buy a platform ticket?"

I lowered my eyes.

"No," I said. "No."

He shook with emotion.

And so did I.

Of such moments is the stock of friendship forged.

I watched him depart the station yard, and as his dear, familiar, bottle-green Humber disappeared from view with half old Squire Brearley's cattle grid and the corpses of three of Grannie Swanton's Buff Orpingtons dangling from its rear bumper I confess I blubbed shamelessly.

I was still in a state of "high emotion" when, fifteen hours later, we reached the landing strip at

Heathrow and boarded the moving aeroplane.

We travelled under conditions of extreme squalor, throughout which the lady wife viewed me with icy disdain.

I tried to make conversation.

"Look," I said, pointing out of the window. "That must be Iceland."

"Humph," said the lady wife.

"Jolly decent of the chaps to live there, don't you think?" I said.

"Humph."

I looked out of the window again and examined more closely the bleak, icy, gale-ravaged wasteland.

"Of course it could always be Old Trafford," I said.

"Humph," said the lady wife and immersed herself once more in her paperback library book entitled "The Official War Office Biography of Sir Geoffrey Boycott – *Volume Seven* – The Years of Destiny, Aged Three to Six and a Half."

Hell.

Sheer, unadulterated hell.

Admit it, dear readers, travel by moving aeroplane is as stimulating as sitting in the middle of a jumbo-sized packet of medicated catarrh pastilles.

The hours dragged by interminably.

Vast legions of infants in arms howled and puked endlessly, for all the world like spectators on the Hill at Sydney Cricket Ground.

I could stand it no longer.

I poked the lady wife in the ribs with the handle of my stumper's mallet and said:

"Well, it can't be long now till we pole up in Australia."

"Australia?" said the lady wife. "Australia? We haven't even landed in America yet."

Oh God, another nail in the coffin.

To my horror it transpired that the lady wife had arranged for us to break our journey at a hell-hole, name of Los Angeles, which in my ignorance I had always assumed was the title of some obscure rhumba band on Workers' Playtime of blessed memory.

Would that it had been, dear readers, would that it had.

Can you imagine my chagrin when I discovered the name of our night's lodgings?

The Beverly Wiltshire!

How typical of the lady wife's atavistic miserliness – the bloody place wasn't even first class.

The Beverly Derbyshire or the Beverly Worcestershire – that might have been acceptable to a lover of our "summer game".

But the Beverly Wiltshire!

Good God, it's only Minor Counties.

I spent a thoroughly wretched night.

What the Yanks don't realise is that the only requirements the true red-blooded Englishman needs for an overnight stay in an hotel is a dry and level space for his palliasse, ample supplies of standing water for his ablutions activities and sufficient bookshelf space for his Wisden's Almanacks.

What he does not need are two bathrooms, twenty-seven multi-coloured telephones, uncountable numbers of shower caps, shoe horns, darning kits, unstrikeable paper matches and a bed the size of Twickenham rugby football pitch.

What a scandalous waste of space and resources.

Dear Lord, in our room I could have accommodated the whole of Fred Rumsey's hindparts and "made a good show" of staging the World Welterweight Boxing Championship.

If there is one race upon this earth I detest above all others it is the Yanks with their ill-fitting shirts and their air-conditioned handshakes.

I am not a prejudiced man, but . . .

We spent the rest of our stay in Los Angeles in a smog-bound torpor.

The lady wife averred that it was "worth it" because she had seen in the foyer of the hotel some starlet of the moving kinematograph screen, name of Ann Hefflin.

I myself did not see the swine.

I did, however, see Sir C. Aubrey Smith, who was looking "in the pink".

And thus did we enplane once more for the "final

leg" of our journey to Australia.

The langorous torpor of Los Angeles mixed pleasurably with a state of semi-intoxication induced by the fumes from the whisky-sodden breaths of the swarms of Australian surfers who boarded the plane at Honolulu and entertained themselves for the rest of the journey by eating the blankets of their fellow travellers.

The lady wife kept the scum at bay with liberal squirtings from her linseed oil anti-mugger spray, and I "did my bit" with the handle of my portable cricket bat.

And so, dear readers, we find ourselves in our winter quarters in Adelaide.

I have passed on the personal regards of Lady Falklander, The Ink Monitor at Number Ten, to Colonel "Mad" Bob Willis and the troops.

As requested I have brought for them a trunkful of Phyllosan for Mr Bob Taylor, a fresh selection of Rupert annuals for Master Derek Pringle and a letter of consolation for the lugubrious Innersole from Sir Geoffrey Boycott.

And now in the dead of the tropic night I sit on the balcony of the hotel launderette and look out on moon-bleached hills, whispering, hissing palms ruffled by the sighs and screams of small birds of the night, and I have only one thing to say:

"I want to go home."

"I want to go home."

THREE

First Impressions

First impressions are "not good".

We have been in Adelaide for three long, weary, dreary, arduous days.

As yet we have shown no signs of scurvy, rickets or trench fever.

We have not been stung by serpent or disembowelled by kangaroo or gored by Robert Hawke.

The lady wife, I am bound to say, has been "confined to quarters" this past two days with a particularly virulent attack of the dreaded Nawab of Pataudis.

That apart, however, the situation is dire indeed.

I am not a prejudiced man, but I say with all sincerity and objectivity that Australia is the open wound of all that is vile and loathesome in the civilized world.

Australia is the dregs at the bottom of the billycan of all that is brutish, loutish and boorish in the behaviour of mankind.

Australia is totally, constantly, unrelievedly beastly.

Do I overstate my case?

I think not.

Consider this – three days we have been here and I have not seen a single quality dry cleaner's shop, "ne'er a trace" of a decent packet of absorbent pipe cleaners, and there seems to be a total absence of dog biscuit shops.

Yes, this is indeed a vile land.

How else to explain the execrable behaviour of the English touring team, in whose hotel, by some ghastly chance of fate, we have found ourselves quartered?

They are young lads in the prime of life, I grant you.

One expects them to be physically "in the pink" and bursting with good humour, high spirits and carnal desires for the collecting of cigarette cards and the breeding of Norwich canaries.

But there must be discipline among the troops, and here I have taken the profoundest exception to the performance of their C.O., Colonel "Mad" Bob Willis.

Colonel Bob has been on many a campaign in foreign climes.

He has personally witnessed the near saintly self-abasement and total unselfishness of the Mahatma Boycott on all his England tours.

With that example shining brightly in his soul there can be no possible excuse for the slackness and indiscipline he has allowed to fester among the ranks.

It is simply "not good enough" for us to have been kept awake all night by Robin Jackman running up and down the hotel corridors practising his appealing.

It is "beyond the bounds" to have to listen to Bob "Juliet Bravo" Taylor serenading Master Pringle to sleep with his ghastly rendition of Christopher Robin.

It might have been faintly tolerable if he'd kept his teeth in.

What was profoundly intolerable was the sound of David Gower doing underwater impersonations of Lulu in the hotel swimming pool at midnight and the indescribable clamour of Norman Cowans' personal steel band accompanying Norman Gifford's limbo dancing in the hotel car park.

The accompanying English journalists and cricket writers are hardly blameless in this matter.

Consider some of the examples of deplorable behaviour I have witnessed:

"Bruce" Woodcock of *The Times* tobogganing down the main staircase of the hotel on his portable typewriter.

Gustav Marlar of the *Sunday Times* jogging round the dining hall at luncheon dressed in nothing but silver lamé jock strap and "I Love Ian Chappell" stickers affixed to his nipples.

And that dreadful little Commie dago, Matthew Engels of the *Guardian*, who has made a totally unhealthy and conspiratorial alliance with Vic "Karl" Marks of the touring team, which explains to me why "certain" cricketers are now demanding a secret ballot before any bowling change takes place on the field of play.

I am convinced, dear readers, you will agree with me that the whole affair was intolerably brutish and that I was perfectly justified in demanding of the hotel manager that he sling the whole lot out of his establishment forthwith.

This he has done.

And I am bound to say that I felt not the slightest pangs of remorse as I watched them shuffling forlornly through the dusty streets, cricket bags balanced precariously on their bowed heads, en route to my old and infinitely valued friend Lord Henry Blofeld's residence, where that noble and kindly soul has promised them quarters in his stables.

How different from the impeccable behaviour of the Australian cricketers, journalists and television commentators, who are also staying at our hotel.

What an example they have set to us all.

Not a drop of hard liquor has passed their lips this past three days.

They have kept themselves constantly busy doing the shopping for the more aged of Adelaide's senior citizens, helping little old ladies and Bob Taylor across the street and taking Master Pringle to the zoo to feed the lions and tigers.

I hesitate to name names, but I do feel a special mention should be made of our dear beloved Fred Trueman, who at great personal sacrifice has volunteered to come Down Under to commentate for the Australian moving television.

Every morning and evening he sits in the foyer of the hotel and his cheery greetings to one and all, and his bright, radiant smile and the infectious tinkle of his happy laughter have done so much to enhance the "party atmosphere".

What a wag he is.

I think, too, of the marvellous Tony Greig, who each morning stands by the door of the breakfast room, distributing food parcels and largesse from his own personal fortune to penurious English cricket supporters, most of whom have travelled thousands of miles from their homeland through steaming jungle, fetid swamp and stinging desert simply in order to kiss his ring.

Nor, of course, would the list be complete without the magnificent Richie Benaud.

Dear, dear Richie.

What a welcome he gave me when I left intelligence in his dinky little pigeon hole that I was staying in the same hotel as he.

He has literally showered me with courtesies and

considerations.

I must be the only man privileged to have seen him "at his toilet" as he bathes himself in asses' milk and sprinkles his exquisite body with that rarest of rare perfumes, Essence of Sproat.

He showed me also his superb and dazzling wardrobe, which is under the personal and constant supervision of the keeper of the Victoria and Albert Museum, Dame Zandra Rhodes, second son of the immortal Wilfred.

But the highest honour of all was when he allowed me to attend the midnight devotions of the Australian cricketers round the hotel consecrated barbecue.

Words cannot describe the ecstacy that overcame me as I listened to the ravishing plainsong of Rodney Marsh and the stirring tones of that finest of all evangelist preachers, the Rev. Dennis Lillee, as he launched into his celebrated sermon:

"Take heed, all ye unbelievers, and listen to how me and Tommo fucked the Poms at Perth."

Unfortunately, however, these are the only "bright spots" on a horizon that stretches before me in an aura of unrelieved gloom.

Yesterday I thought I saw Ernest Wampola, erstwhile accompanist to that fine coloratura soprano and occasional baritone, Dame Tessie O'Shea, but it turned out to be the lugubrious Innersole, manager of the England touring party, and once more I was plunged into the depths of despair.

That gallant and intrepid explorer Lord Henry Blofeld, who single-handedly "opened up" Australia to the western world, has described Adelaide as the most gentle of antipodean cities.

That may well be so.

The city is indeed full of wide and gracious boulevards, elegant parklands and dignified colonial public buildings.

The trouble is that the place is absolutely teeming with Australians.

What scum.

I have to state here and now that as a nation of pet-lovers they are complete "wash-outs".

Everywhere one goes the parks and public places are full of cockatoos and budgerigars, which can mean only one thing – their owners simply cannot be bothered to secure the locks on their pets' cages before retiring to bed.

This irresponsibility of behaviour is well exemplified by the Australians' cavalier attitude towards time.

Here Down Under they do not have time as we know it in the Mother Country.

At an hour when all decent, civilized, animal-loving, sweet-smelling, pink-tongued, clean-navelled Englishmen are safe abed and dreaming sweet dreams of opening the batting for their country with Mr Winston Place, or defacing photographs of Mary O'Hara in the *TV Times*, the loutish, fat-ankled, wizened-skinned Australian is guzzling vast quantities of his weak, tepid beer and stuffing his revolting hairy pot belly with meat pies of the taste, consistency and odour of molten india rubbers.

Again, at a time when the typical Englishman is nibbling delicate wafers of cucumber sandwiches and sipping Earl Grey tea on sun-shimmered, moss-cropped lawns, the foul Australian is snoring and twitching and belching and breaking wind in a bed which has all the charm and comfort of the bottom of a trolley bus inspection pit.

The excuse proffered by the Australian vermin for this nauseating behaviour is "time difference".

Time difference?

Stuff and nonsense!

If the odious square-headed Hun and the greasy stubble-chinned Wop can keep the same time scale as us, so can friend Digger.

Just think how much more convenient it would be for all those concerned with "Two Way Family Favourites" on the talking wireless.

But matters of common courtesy and simple decency do not concern the typical slothful self-satisfied Australian.

Consider my predicament.

Ever since leaving the Mother Country I have been constantly putting my watch backwards and forwards for the sake of the so-called "time zones".

Good God, only yesterday I had to leave the hotel dining room to attend to a call of nature in the ablutions offices, and dear Richie Benaud, eager as always to help, instructed me to put my watch three-quarters of an hour backwards because I was entering a different time zone.

On accomplishing the operation successfully and returning to the room, the divine Richie instructed me to put my watch three-quarters of an hour forward.

Thus through the perverse and artificial vagaries of time are precious moments lost forever to posterity.

I have to report other oddities of behaviour among the natives.

I had occasion on the first day of our sojourn in this vile land to visit the hotel swimming pool, it being the only suitable place to knock out my pipe, and there I read the following notice:

"No person shall spit, spout water, blow his nose or urinate in the pool."

How barbarous.

How typically uncivilized.

For what other reason could a sane man in possession of all his faculties possibly wish to enter a swimming pool?

And so, with the relentless sun beating down, lead in the cockles of my heart and anguish screaming at the nerve ends of my soul, I trudge upstairs once more to attend to the bed-bound lady wife.

Does she need yet another stone hot water bottle?

Does she need more blankets?

Does she need a change of thermal underwear and balaclava?

Well, after all, dear readers, it is Christmas in Australia in three weeks' time.

Christmas, with the sun shining and the mosquitos biting?

I am not a prejudiced man, but . . .

FOUR

A Day Out

Well, the terrifying and monstrous natural disaster which the whole Australian nation has feared this past month has happened at long last.

Yes, the lady wife has recovered from her attack of the dreaded Nawabs.

The subsequent ghastly sequence of events was "set in motion" some two days previously.

Full of joy and tingling anticipation I was about to "sneak out" for a day's foot hunting with Lord Henry Blofeld and the Barossa platypus hounds, when the lady wife appeared in the foyer of the hotel attired in Barbour coat and Free Foresters' leg warmers and announced in those doom-laden hectoring tones so familiar to all those who have attended a press conference given by Lady Falklander:

"I am restored to health. I wish to be taken out."

And she affixed me with those piggy little eyes, which look for all the world like the knot holes in the surface of The Oval gasometer-end sightscreen, and added:

"By you!"

Dear, lovable, cuddly Freddie Trueman, who perchance was sitting in the vicinity crocheting a fountain pen muff for his beloved Mary Poppins-Parkinson, Mother Superior of the Hospice for Distressed Television Interviewers, shook his head sadly, clapped me warmly on the shoulders and said:

"Hard cheddar.

"I were just abaht to invite thee out for a day's brass rubbing wi' Tony Greig and Richie Thingermebob.

"And I tell thee, owd lad, if tha rubs them two together, tha gets more brass than what's in the vaults of t'Yorkshire Trustees Savings Bank."

How I laughed.

What a wag he is.

He is to the wit of cricket what Dame Googly Withers is to the art of tram conducting.

However, such thoughts were swiftly dispelled by the lady wife, who grabbed me by the scruff of the neck, frog-marched me to the telephone and insisted that I book a rental car "there and then".

Much to my dismay it was delivered to our hotel "within the hour" by an Australian female who, to my untutored eyes, appeared to have teeth the shape and colour of second class English postage stamps and a predatory eye which could have filleted a shark at fifteen nautical inches.

I was later to discover that this was typical of the gender the length and breadth of this foul and benighted country.

We set off from the hotel with the lady wife "at the helm" and "yours truly" in his customary role as navigator.

After extricating ourselves with some difficulty from two hypermarket car parks and the main crossing point for the Glenelg-Adelaide tramway, we were soon "bowling along" merrily in the open country.

We paused on two occasions to allow the lady wife to flag down cars which she deemed to have been following too close behind her, and to belabour their drivers about the heads with the handle of her brolly.

How the brutes yelled.

It is, of course, the only way to treat them.

When we return to Blighty I shall, as a matter of principle, soundly thrash every Australian I meet on the street without a word of explanation.

It is my firm opinion that if all my fellow countrymen were to adopt this practice we should soon be rid of these excrescences (as well as the dagos, the Arabs, the Irish, the Maltese and similar foreign scum) and England would once again be a land of freedom and compassion, a haven for the oppressed and persecuted and the victims of rampant prejudice, and our womenfolk could once more walk our streets without fear of being mugged by gangs of drink-crazed Persian shoplifters.

I am not a prejudiced man, but . . .

I was interrupted in my reverie by the lady wife rapping me on the knee with the sharp end of her shooting stick and speaking the following words:

"Rather charming, don't you think?"

"What?" I said.

Once more she rapped me on the kneecap, and this time she hissed through those familiar yellowing equine teeth:

"The scenery, man. The scenery."

I looked around me.

The vile sun blazed down shamelessly from a smug and disgustingly blue sky.

The parched pastures were scarred with groves of eucalyptus, gentle hills were rilled with dry-throated creeks and tin-roofed farmsteads brooded in bleak isolation, to create a picture which looked remarkably like the slag heap country to the south of Grimethorpe colliery.

When I apprised the lady wife of this opinion, she snorted through those familiar porcine nostrils and snapped:

"What do you expect? There's a drought on. They haven't had a drop of rain for fifteen years."

Typical, I thought.

Absolutely typical.

As the sun climbed higher in the heavens the

ghastliness of the scenery increased – the grass grew more scorched and yellow, the forests more stunted and the creeks more barren – and I was about to "nod off", when the lady wife turned the loathesome Nipponese car violently to the left and drove through a gateway, over which were written the following ominous words:

"The Poodunga Wildlife Park and Natural History Museum."

Oh, my God.

If there is one thing I detest more than prunes and custard, damp braces and the cricket reports of Mr Tony Lewis it is zoos.

Why any sane and civilized man should choose to visit a zoo, to be gawped at by legions of grinning monkeys scratching their private parts and sniffing their fingers, is totally beyond me.

It is of no educational value to the monkeys.

They derive no aesthetic satisfaction from it.

It is sheer, wanton cruelty to inflict the misery of a zoo upon a God-fearing, pipe-smoking, ginger plus-foured lover of the "summer game".

Dear Lord, he's an endangered species these days.

These thoughts were brooding in my mind as the lady wife berthed our vehicle and hustled me into the park.

What misery!

The first thing I saw on entering was a giant herd of fossilized Lamingtons browsing in a forest of petrified Vegemite.

Worse was to follow – compound after compound after compound full of examples of the hideous Australian flora and fauna.

If I see another Benaud-billed platypus I swear I shall scream and bite chunks out of the lady wife's golfing socks.

For three solid hours we tramped round the enclosures being screeched at by scaly-breasted Lilleekeets, leaden-toed marsh whistlers, brown-tailed slipcatchers and striated southern hoggrunners.

Finally the lady wife decided with her typical arbitrary repulsiveness that she "had had enough" and we repaired to the car park, found our vehicle and directed it homewards.

All went well for the first two hours, and then a most curious thing happened.

The sky began to cloud over.

A chill wind sprang up from the south.

The trees bent themselves before it.

Black clouds lumbered up over the horizon.

Thunder rumbled.

Lightning flickered.

Darker and darker grew the skies.

Birds cowered.

Sheep shivered.

And then there was a drum-shattering clap of thunder, a brilliant and deafening flash of lightning, and the heavens opened.

How the rain lashed down.

How it coiled and hissed.

We were forced to stop the car and draw into a layby.

The rain pounded on the roof of the car.

It seared across the windscreen.

The wind howled and shrieked.

And then quite suddenly it stopped.

The rain stopped.

The wind stopped.

The clouds disappeared.

The sun returned to its station high in the heavens, and the grass sparkled and new green leaves glistened.

We turned to each other and smiled nervously.

And then I saw them.

Twenty or thirty black men rising from a crop of scrubby bushes and commencing to crawl on all fours towards us.

Their eyes were bloodshot and wild.

Their teeth were yellow and snarling.

Their bodies twitched and their flat noses snorted.

Dear God, they looked for all the world like the BBC ball-by-ball commentary team waiting for the luncheon adjournment at Lords.

In a panic the lady wife went for the starter.

No use.

It spluttered and coughed.

Nearer and nearer came the black men.

More and more frantically did the lady wife attempt to start the car.

In vain.

The leader of the pack reached our car and, leaping up in the air with a hideous cry of triumph, wrenched open the door of the driver's seat and dragged out the lady wife.

I confess I thought we were "done for".

I prepared myself for the worst and closed my eyes.

In the space of a fraction of a second my past life flashed before my eyes, my most precious memories flooded before me – post-lunch snorters with the Commodore in his summer house at Witney Scrotum, taking a net with Dame Vera Lynn, dining by moonlight with Gordon Garlick, sharing a bench at the chiropodist's with Cyril Washbrook.

When I opened my eyes again, a most singular sight presented itself to me.

The black men were grouped in a circle round the lady wife.

She was standing there motionless and calm, her umbrella held aloft in her right hand.

And she was naked!

Oh God, I thought.

Not that.

Not . . .

I leapt out of the car and raced towards the savages.

"Don't, don't. For God's sake, don't," I cried, pointing at the naked lady wife. "You fools. Don't touch her. You don't know what you're taking on."

The leader of the black men motioned me to silence.

There was a dignity to his mien and a softness to his features which forced me to comply instantly.

And then he spoke, addressing himself to the lady wife.

"We have waited for you, oh great white mother from across the boundless oceans.

"For fifteen long and parched years we have waited for you to come to us.

"We knew one day you would, for so it is written in the turds of kangaroos and the toenail parings of Ian Chappell.

"Oh, great white mother, you have brought us rain.

"After fifteen long hard years of drought and hardship you have brought the big black clouds that spew out their bellies and drown our parched and wilted land.

"We praise thee.

"We salute thee.

"We worship thee."

And thus did the party of rude and innocent aboriginals begin to dance.

They circled round the lady wife, stamping their feet, rolling their eyes and clicking their tongues for all the world like lady spectators queuing to get into the Warner stand on the Saturday of the Lords Test.

The lady wife stabbed her umbrella at me and indicated that I should join the dance.

This I did.

For a few moments I own I felt "a bit of chump" in my plus fours and MCC panama hat, but after a while I entered "into the spirit of things" and was soon wailing and stomping with the best of them.

"All right, all right," said the lady wife.

"There's no need to overdo it."

The dance went on for two hours and at length the black brutes flopped to the ground exhausted.

After a while they smiled at us shyly and then they offered us food and drink – slow-roasted slug, worm casserole, cricket bag fritters, all washed down with liberal quantities of shirt-tail gin.

It was the finest fare we had had to date Down Under.

We did not leave until sundown, when we departed after a ceremony at which we were made blood brothers of the tribe.

How moving it was as the simple, unsophisticated aboriginals pricked our skin with the corners of their American Express credit cards and mingled our blood with theirs.

Not a word did we say as we drove home.

Not a word did we say as we flopped exhausted into the conjugal container.

And while the hours ticked by into the dead of the tropic night I turned to the lady wife as she lay in the deepest of deep slumbers, and the vision of her standing naked in the middle of the circle of black men flashed into my mind, and I thought one of the profoundest thoughts I have ever entertained:

"By God, I never knew she'd got such hairy legs."

FIVE

Before The Match

There is one activity which to lovers of the "summer game" takes precedence above all others.

I do not refer to armpit sniffing.

I do not refer to collecting the gramophone records of Charlie Kunz, embroidering romper suits for Derek Pringle, knitting maroon ear muffs for Alec Bedser, buying hearing aids and contact lenses for Australian umpires, or creeping up softly behind cats and then suddenly jumping up, shouting and waving one's arms so violently that the brutes are frightened out of their mean-livered wits and flee to the Commodore's garden, where they are damn near pecked to death by his geese.

No.

I refer to foreplay.

Foreplay!

How the juices tingle and the passions rumble at the mention of that word.

The knees weaken, the temples throb and there is unaccustomed movement in the nether regions of the popping crease.

Foreplay!

The slow build up, the anticipation, the deliberate prolonging of the climactic crescendo of uncontrolled carnality – yes, dear readers, those two hours before the start of a cricket match are indeed the ultimate sublimeness of the human experience.

Who in their right mind could have imagined that here in Australia the verminous, gross-featured, intolerant, pock-skinned natives should also have been privy to this highest peak of rapture and ecstacy?

But indeed they have.

It grieves me to say it, but here at the Adelaide Oval Cricket Ground there are vestiges of life "as we know it" in the Mother Country.

I have seen cricket grounds in many continents and in many climes.

I have seen Buxton under snow in the height of summer.

I have seen typhoon and tempest at Old Trafford.

I have seen Headingly stricken by plague and The Oval ravaged by drought and famine.

I have seen the sun go down in a fiery tropical glow behind the minarets and soaring buttresses of our beloved Bramall Lane.

And, yes, I have seen the sun go down behind the soaring buttresses of Mr Ken Higgs at Grace Road.

But never ever have I seen a cricket ground as beautiful as the Adelaide Oval.

The ground is ringed by massed ranks of trees – gaunt and angular Lawry pines, exotic Benaud bushes aflame with blossom and dental floss, stately Jardine oaks and the weirdly contorted Packer palms, known more familiarly as "the banknote tree".

Dominating one corner of this lovely monument to all that is finest in our beloved "summer game" is the cathedral of St Norman and St Slasher, in whose sanctum can be found some of the holiest relics of Australian cricket.

With hushed reverence, pilgrims from all over the world come to admire and worship the umpire's coat which bears the stigmata of Mr Dennis Lillee's front incisors, the cask which legend says contains a death mask of Mr Ian Chappell's wallet and, holiest of holiest, the tape on which is recorded the very first radio commentary made to the Australian nation by Lord Henry Blofeld.

Yes, at Adelaide Oval every prospect pleases.

Silver gulls soar lazily, hazily round the pavilion spires.

Willy-wagtails flick and flitter on the lush greensward.

Gentle breezes waft from the nearby Murray River, named of course after the former Middlesex and England stumper, John, who discovered the watercourse during the "rest day" of the Adelaide Test of '66.

I am provoked into these fond reflections by memories of my attendance at the first day of the Adelaide Test during our tour Down Under.

Taking a tip from the repulsive natives I arrived early in order to "stake out" my place.

By nine o'clock in the morning I was already ensconced with camping chair, shooting stick, luncheon basket, waterproof leggings and inflatable binoculars in an advantageous spot in a corner of the pavilion bar.

I was "not a moment too early".

Within the hour the bar was "heaving" with the sweating, cursing, belching, nose-picking typical upper-class Australians, all clamouring for the waiters to insert into their mouths the hose pipes with which the scum in this part of the world dispense their weak and tepid beer, thus hastening the condition of terminal drunkenness which appears to be endemic in these climes.

I bore it stoically for a while, but having been damn near decapitated by an "eskie" wielded by some hairy-chested, splay-footed lout, who bore a marked resemblance to Miss Joan Sutherland, I decided I could stand it no longer.

Cleaving a way with my stumper's mallet through the staggering, lurching, beer-swilling, smoke-shrouded bar, which looked for all the world like a Hogarth print of an Aldgate gin palace, or an aquatint of the inside of the Australian dressing room, I stumbled out into the fresh air.

What bliss.

What relief.

After regaining my breath and sheathing the stumper's mallet down the right leg of my plus fours I looked about me.

It was indeed a most pleasing vision.

On the green, springy lawns there were marquees and stalls where tail-coated waiters dispensed strawberries and cream and fine menthol-flavoured wines from the Barossa valley. Facing them were small compounds wherein were coralled Test Match cricketers from days gone by.

For the sum of two Australian dollars one could purchase a bag of buns or broken biscuits with which to feed the poor brutes.

A nice touch this, I thought, as I wandered up and down the lines smiling at dear old "Plum" Warner "minding his bike" as usual with Victor Trumper, who was looking in marvellous health, and K. S. Ranjitsinhji, who was hard at work baking curried cricket balls in his tandoori oven.

I idly tossed a rum-impregnated digestive biscuit to Mr Keith Miller and watched with pleasure as the poor wretch scrabbled for it in the dust with a wild-maned, nostril-hissing, spitting and snarling figure, which I first took to be a Tasmanian Devil, but which later turned out to be Mr Ian Chappell.

Warmed in spirit by the sight of these two heroes

of the past, and comforted in the knowledge that the "authorities" were caring so well for Mr Chappell in his dotage, I strolled towards the nets.

Familiar faces!

There was dear stoop-shouldered Vic Marks carrying Monsignor Tavare's cricket bag and portable confirmation kit, with his familiar expression of someone who has just been told he is to spend the rest of his life as a junior lecturer in soap technology.

And there, scowling ferociously at the fast bowling machine, was tiny, perfectly-formed Alan Lamb, looking remarkably like a National Hunt jockey who has once again been "warned off" at Bangor-on-Dee.

It was good to see "the lads" in such good shape.

I feel that it has much to do with the extensive financial sponsorships they have received.

These, I am certain, have relieved them of many of the monetary burdens which have so plagued touring teams of the past and were, I am convinced, responsible for the mass outbreaks of shoplifting, pickpocketing and bed-wetting which gave English teams abroad such "a bad reputation".

The team is, in its entirety, I believe, sponsored by a Nip organization specializing in the manufacture of digital scorecard printing presses and electronic umpires.

There are, of course, individual sponsorships,

among which we find Master Derek Pringle sponsored by Mothercare, Mr Derek Randall by Oxfam and Mr Bob Taylor by Help the Aged.

I beamed with pleasure as I watched Colonel "Mad" Bob Willis put them through their paces.

But then there occurred something most singular and disturbing.

The sun was blotted out.

Birds stopped singing.

An icy blast of wind shivered the trees.

My teeth chattered.

The hair stood up on the back of my neck.

I turned.

Yes, as I expected, it was Alec Bedser passing by.

As soon as he disappeared the sun returned, and the gaudy-hued parrakeets resumed their fruitless quest to outscreech Robin Jackman.

It was then that I heard once more those dear familiar crystal and clarion tones ringing out clearly above the adenoidal whine of the nicotine-stained Aussies.

"My dear old thing, how lovely to see you. You must come and take French champagne in my personal marquee."

Yes, it was my old chum, Lord Henry Blofeld.

He strode towards me, his monocle flashing most fearfully as he beat off the hordes of female admirers with the flat of his trusty sabre, and he embraced me warmly.

"My dear old thing," he said. "Isn't Australia simply too beastly for words?

"I've only come here to save it from Michael Parkinson.

"Fearful, jumped-up little stinker. Married to the official nanny to the English team, don't you know."

He escorted me to his personal marquee, striped with the colours of MCC and aflutter with his personal standards and battle-flags, and there, seated on cushions of purest shantung silk, embroidered with the colours of Boodles and Eton college, we sipped French champagne and Lord Henry "filled me in" on the latest gossip from home. As usual he was the perfect host.

His liveried flunkies attended to us silently and efficiently.

The service of his unctuous and wheedling bed pan wallah, who incidentally bore a marked resemblance to Mr Tony Lewis, was beyond reproach.

And I particularly enjoyed the singing of his personal choir of castrati, all, I was assured, former members of the BBC ball-by-ball radio commentary team.

Presently Lord Henry stood up and excused himself.

"Frightful bore, old thing," he said. "Must go.

"Got to open the state parliament.

"Won't be a jiff."

And he smiled and discreetly pressed a bag of gold sovereigns into my hand.

What an urbane and civilized man, I thought as I left his compound, with its Sikh guards standing stiffly to attention, and made my way to the front of the pavilion, from which vantage point I watched the drunken antics of the slobbering louts by the scoreboard.

What scum!

What vileness.

It was their habit to amuse their minute, shrivelled and wasted minds by baying and howling every time a pretty Australian girl passed in front of them.

Thankfully this was not a frequent occurrence.

I was about to turn away from them when I was prodded in the ribs by a small man wearing navy blue suit, brown boots, white silk muffler and flat cap.

He took out his false teeth and addressed me in the unmistakable slack-jawed, catarrh-clogged tones of the North of England.

"Are you a Pom?" he said.

"No, I most certainly am not," I said. "I am an Englishman. English, English, English — that's what I am. Don't you understand that, you brute?"

He smiled.

"That's right," he said. "I thought you was a Pom."

He looked at me and smiled again, and it occurred to me that he was probably begging for alms.

I was about to "slip him" one of my newly-acquired gold sovereigns when he prodded me in the ribs once more and "launched himself" into the following monologue:

"What do you think to the Australians?

"Load of shite, aren't they?

"Bastards!

"I've lived over here seventeen year come Eastertide.

"I wouldn't go back to Crumpsall for all the rice in China.

"I bloody would not.

"I tell you – the only thing wrong with Australia is the bloody Aussies.

"Bastards!

"I have nothing to do with them.

"Do I hell as like.

"I never mix with them.

"Do I buggery.

"I go to Pommie clubs and Pommie pubs.

"I wouldn't give you half a crown for the Aussies.

"Look at them.

"Have you ever seen so many fat people in the whole of your life?

"Bastards.

"And I'll tell you another thing – don't eat their meat pies.

"They're rubbish.

"Take one bite out of them and you're covered from back collar stud to your boots in gravy.

"Bastards!

"And here's another tip.

"Never wear short trousers in the garden.

"If you wear short trousers in the garden, you'll be bitten to buggery by bull ants.

"Bastards!

"And I'll tell you something else about Australians.

"Never let your daughter marry one.

"Mine has.

"Bastard.

"All he thinks about is booze, gambling and women – in that order.

"And I'll tell you another thing about him – he's a cheat at sport, he eats like a pig and he's got a foul mouth.

"Bastard.

"Now my other daughter – she married the Chinaman.

"What a bloody difference.

"He'll do anything for you, will the Chinaman.

"His table manners are tip top and he's shit hot at making fitted wardrobes.

"Aye, he's a gent, is the Chinaman.

"Not like the Aussies.

"Take my tip and don't have nothing to do with

them while you're here, or you'll be contaminated for life.

"Bastards!"

And with that he tipped the peak of his cap to me and disappeared into the crowd with a jaunty lilt to his gait.

I smiled to myself warmly.

How good it was to hear the voice of English sweet reason and common sense rising triumphantly above the clamour of prejudice and base intolerance.

Oh, the heady delights of those magical, blissful moments "before the match".

There is only one thing that spoils them for me – the knowledge that sooner or later I've got to sit down and actually watch the bloody game.

SIX

First Dispatches
From The Front

During the course of my long, wearisome and infinitely painful exile Down Under it was my custom to send regular dispatches to my dear friend, the Commodore, at his residence in Witney Scrotum.

I have to confess that I am not "one of nature's letter writers".

I have not the instinctive grace and facility of the immortal E. R. "Elizabeth Regina" Dexter.

I quote from one of his earliest but finest of letters:

"Dear Mam,

"Me and the lads are having a smashing time at camp. Akela makes smashing sausages and chips on the camp fire and they're smashing to drink Vimto with but you mustn't shake the bottle or all the fizz comes out of your nose when you drink it."

How exquisite!

How exquisite, too, the noble narrative skills of E. W. "Gloria" Swanton.

I quote a favourite item from his celebrated

personal anthology entitled, "Letters to the Mother Country."

"Your Majesty,

"We arrived at Perth, from which place we journied most arduously to Brisbane, wherefrom we entrained to Adelaide, fromwhence we embarked to Melbourne, whencefrom we peregrinated to Sydney, hencefromwhich we . . ."

How Queen Victoria must have thrilled to that missive from her most loyal and humble of subjects.

But back to my letter writing.

My attitude to the art is pragmatic – I consider it to be a thundering bloody nuisance best left to spinster ladies of "mature years", adolescent shop girls with acne and dandruff corresponding with actors from the moving kinematograph, and newsagents threatening to sue the lady wife unless she pays her paper bill within three days.

Why, therefore, was I persuaded to "put pen to paper" and correspond with the Commodore?

The answer is simple.

First, the kindly old nautical soul was petrified that whilst Down Under I should be eaten by aboriginals, fatally knocked down by a moving tramcar, or declared a world wildlife heritage zone, and thus did he beg me to write to him weekly to assure him that I was "in the rudest of rude".

Second, knowing my previous experience in the craft of journalism, he asked me to send him daily reports of the progresses of the Test Matches so that he would be given "the true picture".

You may be surprised, dear readers, to learn of my journalistic endeavours.

Well, when a man serves his King and Country in distant climes in every outpost of our far-flung and noble Empire he has to be able to "turn his hand" to anything.

Whilst serving in Burma, for example, during the mass outbreak of sightscreen desecration, I spent several happy months working for the *Rangoon Weekly Clarion and Trumpeter* as assistant lacrosse correspondent.

Experiences like this enabled me to view with sympathy and compassion the desperate plight of the English journalists reporting the course of the England tour Down Under.

Any suggestion that the gibberish, inaccuracy and total incompetence of their reports is caused by drunkenness, excessive womanising or downright dishonesty in the search for a "hot story" is totally without foundation.

I have seen them "at first hand" and can vouch that a more conscientious and clean-living set of fellows it would indeed be difficult to find.

The reason for the incompetent drivel of their reports is simple – the deplorable conditions under which they are forced to work.

Constantly kept short of money by miserly,

tight-fisted, drunken sports editors, they are forced to eke out their meagre finances by baby-sitting for their Australian colleagues, eating the cheapest of synthetic foods and staying in the meanest of lodging houses, where they are kept awake all night by the drunken groans and retchings of itinerant Australian television commentators.

Then, when they get to the cricket ground to report the matches, conditions are even worse.

I have seen them from the privileged vantage point of Lord Henry Blofeld's personal press box, which is transported from ground to ground by a special train guarded by detachments of Ghurkas and Australian naval gunners.

What a pathetic sight they made as we looked down on them in the dark subterranean pit which served as their press box.

Deprived of food and drink from the moment they are locked in at start of play until they are released at "stumps", they are forced to rely for sustenance on the scraps of caviare and smoked gerbils dropped to them from time to time by Lord Henry.

Indeed, at Perth several of them were reduced to eating the homing pigeons which are the only means of transmitting their reports back to head office.

Is it any wonder, therefore, that their work is so execrable?

How my heart bled for them as I sat in Lord

Henry's box being massaged by dusky maidens in transparent wellingtons and lulled by the gentle clapper-clap-clap as the old family typewriter wallah pursued his ancient crafts.

I thought particularly of the agonies borne so bravely by Mr Frith, editor of *Wisden's Cricket Monthly*, by Mr Christopher Martin-Jenkins, editor of *The Cricketer*, by that splendid wit and sophisticate, Mr Jim Laker, by the cricket correspondent of the BBC moving television service, by the chief cricket writer of the *Daily Telegraph* and, of course, by our beloved "Bruce" Woodcock of *The Times* – all known affectionately by lovers of "the summer game" as Dave, C, Dozy, Blaikie, Mick and Tich.

And so, dear readers, if through the medium of these dispatches I can "put the picture straight" I shall feel I have repaid a debt of gratitude to these near saintly "gentlemen of the press", whose selflessness and devotion to duty were such an inspiration to myself, the lugubrious Innersole and Colonel "Mad" Bob Willis and the troops.

Thus do I present the first of my "dispatches from the front" written during those stirring and frustrating days of the Adelaide Test.

THE FIRST DAY

What carnage!

What massacre!

What humiliation!

Serve the English right, I say.

If Colonel "Mad" Bob Willis chooses quite wantonly to spurn the help of the lady wife, then more fool him.

Good God, I told him plainly and clearly that she was "at his disposal" night or day.

I actually sent her into the English dressing room, an hour before the match started, to deliver her celebrated and much-feared "battle speech".

Big, burly Sarn't Major Botham emerged from the dressing room after only five minutes, reeling, ashen-faced and fiddling nervously with the ties of his corset, and even loyal, placid Bob "Juliet Bravo" Taylor lurched out shaking his old grey head and asking in a weak little voice for a change of Thermogene.

The success of the operation seemed assured.

And then what happened?

The England skipper won the toss and put the Australian vermin in to bat.

The lady wife specifically ordered him not to.

She knew as well as the next man that Australian cricket teams should always be compelled to field first.

And why?

Because like all their loathsome, hairy-nostrilled, yellow-tongued fellow countrymen they suffer from endemic and terminal hangovers during the hours of morning, and thus any batsman with an ounce of spunk in him should be able to score at least one hundred and fifty runs before the luncheon adjournment.

Enough of that, however.

Let me state that apart from the confounded nuisance of having to watch the cricket I found my day at the Adelaide Oval thoroughly agreeable.

It is just like dear old Lords – disgusting food, screeching jet planes, far too many Australians and hordes of shaven-haired rabble strutting round the ground with Union Jacks tied round their waists.

What scum!

If I had my way, I should disembowel them on the spot and then publicly suck them to death with Mr Richie Benaud's mouth.

If any of them survived, I should inflict on them the most barbarous torture known to mankind – compulsory attendance at the Sir Geoffrey Boycott annual memorial lecture, which the great man delivers thrice weekly at highly competitive rates during the close season.

So now it's back to our bleak hotel and "Bruce" Woodcock's celebrated home-made corn plaster gin, in the knowledge that if the slaughter continues I shall be forced to insist that the lady wife plays in the next Test.

Thank God, I had the foresight to pack her MCC spats and her Barbara Cartland autographed jock strap.

THE SECOND DAY

I have to report grave news.

This very day the lady wife made specific mention of her loathesome unmarried spinster brother, Naunton.

In my innocence I had thought she had forgotten the existence of this odious creature and banished him from her mind in a malodorous haze of meat pies and "Fishermen's Friends".

No such luck.

As we sat in the temperance champagne marquee at the rear of the pavilion the lady wife "made her plans" for the visitation.

Dear God, under those circumstances how could any civilized man concentrate on a game of cricket?

I have "nothing to report".

THE THIRD DAY

The agony continues!

Despite all the noble exertions of tiny, perfectly-formed Alan Lamb and the aristocratic "hauteur" of

Captain The Hon. David Gower of the 4th Leicester Lancers, we are, I fear, "done for".

Why?

What has gone wrong?

Why is the team in such a state of disarray?

The answer came to me in the tranquil watches of the night.

In a blinding flash was revealed to me the root cause of all our troubles.

It is in one word – Gifford.

What insanity to give the vital position of assistant team manager to a man whose sole claim to fame is as a trainer of moving race horses.

Thus can be explained all our failures and all our disasters.

Dear old "Josh" Gifford just has not the experience of dealing with thoroughbred, highly-strung Test Match cricketers.

Good God, only this morning I caught him trying to fix bit and bridle to Graeme Fowler and attempting to "hobday" the exquisitely-featured Ian Gould.

Then, a few moments later in the nets, I caught the miserable blighter forcing great dollops of hay and pony nuts down the throat of a bewildered Norman Cowans.

No wonder the chap is in such distress.

It's bad enough being stared at constantly by Alec Bedser without suffering the indignity of Bernard

Thomas plaiting and ribbonning your hair every time you go out to bowl.

The man I feel most sorry for is Colonel "Mad" Bob Willis, who has suffered most grievously from Gifford's attentions.

Yes, we all know he's getting "a bit slow round the field" but that is no excuse for firing his fetlocks and having him "tubed".

Thank God, Gifford forgot to pack his gelding irons.

Finally consider the case of Sarn't Major Botham.

He has not "come up to expectations".

And why?

It is not overweight.

It is not lack of commitment.

It is a classic case of fatigue.

Well, wouldn't you feel exhausted having to "muck out" Derek Randall's bedroom every morning?

THE FOURTH DAY

More mention of Naunton.

The lady wife grows daily more excited at the prospect of the meeting.

As for myself, I view the whole proceedings with profound wretchedness.

No wonder the cricket this day has been unrelievedly ghastly.

THE FINAL DAY

Well, it is all over.

Defeat.

Disaster.

Abject disgrace.

How my blood boils and curdles when I think of the wasted effort I have put in supporting the cause.

When I read yesterday in the loathesome Australian gutter press that Colonel "Mad" Bob Willis was complaining that the English batsmen had no experience against an all-out speed attack, my response was instantaneous.

Cuffing the cowardly scum round the earholes with the "sharp end" of my stumper's mallet I herded them into the nets to face the lady wife at her deadliest.

By God, she generated a fearsome head of speed.

The English batsmen were hopping all over the place.

She hurled bouncers at Botham, beamers at Gower and damn near garrotted Sapper Randall with the back-draught from her armpits.

She had no need to bowl at Master Pringle.

She just glared at him and the poor booby fled from the nets, whimpering softly.

Unfortunately her exertions brought a certain amount of discomfort.

Despite the fact that during the whole of her bowling stint she was wearing Barbour coat and lime-green Wellington boots, her nose was caught most hideously by the sun.

Colonel Bob said there was only one thing that would protect it from further exposure – Ian Botham's abdominal protector. Even that massive and titanic structure, however, was not sufficient to cover completely her nasal protuberance.

That apart, it has been a most agreeable day, made even more pleasant by meeting old and cherished friends.

I saw Alec Bedser, who was looking thoroughly pleased with himself having just won, despite intense competition, the Eric Bedser Lookalike Competition.

Richie Benaud, however, was looking decidedly miffed.

In the Richie Benaud Lookalike Competition he had come only second.

The winner was ET.

And now for Melbourne.

I have commissioned the lady wife to supervise the departure of Colonel "Mad" Bob's baggage train.

We simply cannot afford to lose any more of Monsignor Tavare's baptismal catching cradles.

SEVEN

Kingsley Kunzel

Well, we are arrived in Melbourne.

I am not a person given to exaggeration or hyperbole, but I can state without fear of contradiction that never ever in the whole of my life have I felt such extremes of deprivation or such depths of homesickness.

I have to confess in all honesty that we were warned often enough about this malodorous city, with its bone-scouring Antarctic gales and its pot-bellied shop assistants with fat ankles and chunks of butter beneath their fingernails.

Lord Henry Blofeld pleaded with us to join his Christmas houseparty on the royal yacht, on which he had served so gallantly during the Falkland Islands campaign, and which, on the instigation of Lady Falklander, had been presented to him for his own personal use in perpetuity by a grateful nation.

"My dear old things," he said. "I have the most divine cabin for you. It's part of the honeymoon suite used by Princess Margaret during her honeymoon with Irving Rosewater and our beloved Bill

Frindall."

But the lady wife "would not be told".

She remembered what dear Miss Roebuck from the dog biscuit shop had told her six months previously, in the travel agent's at Keating New Town.

"Oh, myself and Miss Rose and Miss Slocombe had a smashing time in our hotel at Melbourne," she said. "We saw Michael Parkinson three times daily, and every morning we had breakfast in bed, and it was brought to us in our own personal bedroom each morning before lunch by this gorgeous waiter with the lovely liquid brown eyes who looked just like that sexy Colin Dredge only he'd got nicer feet."

And so we found ourselves incarcerated in the squalid Benaud Regency International Towers, on whose menus the words "sweet tea biscuits" did not exist, and in whose lifts we were assailed on all sides by hordes of gibbering, grinning Nips clutching to their minute oriental bosoms digital Christmas trees and electronic yuletide logs.

How I longed for home.

How I longed for all those people and all those institutions that make England so great and so civilized and the lack of which make Australia so vile and so incurably second-rate.

I refer, of course, to Gwen Catley, "the Welsh nightingale".

I refer to Doctor Crock and his Crackpots, the chalk streams of Wiltshire, the rushing becks of Lakeland, the rich black loam of the Fen country, Louise Botting, the lazy beer of Dorset, the Radio Revellers, Troise and his Mandoliers, mill chimneys, thatched cottages, drop handlebars, Bill Sowerbutts, washable ink, Archbishop Fred Rumsey, fretwork magazine racks, tyre levers, the Television Toppers, Ernie Roderick, rolling Pennine moors, Airedale terriers, Raymond Glendenning, W. Barrington Dalby, herb gardens, chocolate-flavoured laxatives, Ordnance Survey maps of Wales and the Marches, tomato sandwiches, Gordon Garlick, Kitty Bluett, Syd Patterson, Arie Van Vliet, Vic Oliver, Big Bill Campbell and his Rocky Mountain Rhythm, The Maple Leaf Four, Bill Kerr, Peter Dawson and Chips Rafferty.

What dear, dear people.

What noble institutions.

And how damnably lonely I felt as I thought of them, brooding in the gloomy bleakness of our hotel bedroom.

I was in such extremes of desperation that even the company of the lady wife would have been bearable for the odd minute or two.

But with typical lack of consideration she was once more confined to bed with yet another attack of the dreaded Nawabs, brought about this time by contact with an infected luggage rack on the night

Overland Express from Adelaide to Melbourne.

And so in search of consolation and refreshment I descended to the bar, and thus began my "adventure", which was to lead me ultimately to solving one of the most baffling mysteries known to the "summer game".

I was sitting in a corner, "minding my own business" with a glass of Château McGilvray alcohol-free burgundy, when a most singular incident occurred "before my very eyes".

Into the bar there strode a small, wiry man with snow-white hair and tanned complexion, immaculately dressed in bottle green blazer, light grey flannel trousers and navy blue and white golfing shoes.

He ordered a quadruple brandy and beetroot juice, downed it in a single gulp and instantly collapsed to the floor, from whence he began to froth at the mouth and groan most hideously.

I leapt to my feet and rushed to his assistance.

"I shouldn't bother," said the barman, placidly picking the scab off a boil on the back of his neck. "It's only him."

How could I not bother?

The man was obviously in the direst of dire straits.

Although he was patently of Australian origin, he did have the right to be accorded a few of the basic decencies of civilized human behaviour, and even if

I could not help I felt certain there was someone in the hotel capable of "putting him down" humanely and painlessly.

I approached him with extreme caution.

Having served in the remotest and most savage outposts of Empire, I knew only too well the dangers and perils faced by unwary hunters when dealing with prey they assumed to be dead.

I remembered one celebrated huntsman and sportsman from Southern Rhodesian "days" who was most savagely bitten on the right buttock by his wife, whom he was in the process of interring after having seen her struck a violent blow on the left temple by a cricket ball propelled by Mr Colin Bland.

In my opinion the chap had every right to assume instant death after such an occurrence.

Typically, his lady wife thought otherwise and insisted on making the most distasteful and vulgar scene.

My chum listened to her silently for a while and then said:

"Well, if you're not dead at least you've been comprehensively run out."

With these memories in mind I ventured closer to the prostrate figure on the cockatoo skin carpet.

It was difficult to decide whether life was indeed "extinct", but as I had encountered this problem previously with so many other Australians I decided to "take a chance".

I began to fan him with the brim of my panama hat.

Nothing.

I prodded him with the blunt end of my stumper's mallet.

Nothing.

I attempted mouth to mouth resuscitation with the miniature jump leads and stirrup pump adaptor I normally keep on my person "in case of emergency".

All to no avail.

There was only one thing for it.

I launched myself at the brute and peppered his rib cage violently with the toes of my boots.

The effect was as remarkable as it was instantaneous.

He opened his eyes.

He smiled broadly.

And he spoke the following words:

"Thanks a lot, old sport. Mine's a treble rum and bilberry."

Before I could respond the barman had poured out the nauseous libation, which the green-blazered creature despatched down his gullet with an expression of sublime content on his face.

For a moment I was speechless.

Then I turned to the barman, who was contentedly scratching the crack of his backside with an india rubber swizzle stick, and said:

"Who is this?"

The barman smiled smugly.

"Stone the crows, you *must* be a stranger," he said.

"Of course I'm a stranger," I said. "It's the only way to cope with living in this godforsaken country. Now who the devil is this creature?"

At this the barman spoke two words, which were to engrave themselves indelibly on my heart and change the whole course of my stay Down Under.

"Kingsley Kunzel," he said.

Kingsley Kunzel!

In the annals of Wisden his name reigns supreme. I quote:

"Most centuries scored whilst drunk . . . Kingsley Kunzel . . . 17."

"Most inebriated batsman to have been given out 'seen the ball twice'. . . Kingsley Kunzel."

Kingsley Kunzel!

How well I recalled the Australian tour of '21, when, after the luncheon adjournment in the match against Derbyshire at Chesterfield, he was given out "sick hit wicket . . . 33".

With what pleasure I conjured up memories of the opening match against Worcestershire, when, despite suffering most grievously from the effects of Ansell's Tummy, he was able with the help of three runners and an auxiliary stretcher bearer to score an undefeated double century before opening time.

And, joy of joys, there he was lying at my feet blithely sipping a quadruple gin and lung tonic.

I took him tenderly by the armpits, raised him upright and with the aid of the barman strapped him to the barstool with my MCC suspenders.

His gratitude was pathetic to behold.

He flung his arms round my shoulders, kissed me thrice on the cheeks, and, after consuming a large vodka and vegemite, whispered in my ear:

"You want to see something, Pommie? You want to see something really exciting?"

I confess to feelings of some alarm, for a similar query some years previously in Port Said had resulted in my witnessing a dusky lady of indeterminate years and sex performing the most extraordinary contortions with a composition cricket ball and half a disused thigh pad, which was to alter drastically and forever my attitude towards fielding practice.

However, curiosity and overpowering boredom with my lot overcame my suspicions, and I allowed myself to be led by my new-found chum to his 5-litre Hispano-Pilling open tourer.

We drove at a furious and ghastly pace for some three hours, and then, after emerging from the hotel car park, headed off to the Dandanong Hills where three days previously the lady wife and I had enjoyed a strenuous day's "abo" shooting with the

Australian Minister for Native Affairs.

The road narrowed as we reached the first foothills, and as we climbed higher the air became chill and the scents of the eucalyptus wreathed and writhed in our nostrils.

My friend drove with reckless abandon, sucking constantly at a rubber pipe which was attached to a brass tap in the dashboard.

He smiled at me.

"Whisky and linseed oil," he said. "Straight from the engine."

And then we turned off the main road into a narrow, grassed and rutted track.

I confess that it was at that moment that I felt the first shivers of apprehension.

Why?

Was it the long, thin, banshee Jackman-like howl of agony that came from the impenetrable and brooding depths of the tangled trees that stooped over the track?

Was it the pile of rotting cricket bags glimpsed through an opening in the forest wall?

Was it the gibbet from which hung a half-eaten stumper's glove?

Was it the human skull affixed to the handle of a Gray-Nicoll five-star "Crusader" cricket bat and standing sentinel at the side of a rotting cabin trunk, out of whose lid there hung the unmistakeable shape of a pair of MCC arch supports?

I had little time to consider these matters, for suddenly we were brought to a shuddering halt by the appearance of a road block.

Immediately we were surrounded by a score of ruffianly figures dressed in yellow trousers and shirts with green piping, and wearing on their heads visored helmets.

They thrust into our faces Duncan Fearnley three-springer sub-machine guns and demanded to know the reason for our presence, but on recognizing Kingsley Kunzel they jumped to attention and waved us on with the most abject and grovelling of apologies, very much in the manner of Tony Greig's farewell speech to Sussex County Cricket Club.

My chum chuckled softly to himself and within a minute we had crested a small brow, and there below was a sight that made my heart miss a beat and caused my plus fours to throb most violently.

Yes, I had seen this monstrous vision many times before in newspaper, magazine and lending library book, but never in my wildest, sweat-soaked nightmares had I imagined that I would actually "see it in the flesh".

But there, in a clearing of the primeval, virgin forest, it stood in all its ghastly horrendousness – the home of the infamous Croaker Brothers, Warren Junior, Ashley and Sydney-Pete.

Some buildings have at their core an unmistakeable sublime goodness, a radiance of honey-tinted tranquillity – here we think automatically of the pavilion at our beloved Bramall Lane.

Other buildings have a gentle mellowness, a gracious calm, like the Harry Makepeace memorial bike sheds at Old Trafford.

Others greet the viewer with a bleak snarl of cruelty, and at their heart broods an evil of incalculable ghastliness – here we think of Colditz Castle and the front of the Oval pavilion.

Such a building was the residence of the Croaker brothers, which I approached on foot with extreme trepidation.

Kingsley Kunzel squeezed my arm warmly.

"No need to worry, blue," he said. "I'm the curator here."

And then he pointed upwards with a cheery smile.

I looked up.

My God.

There, high above on the battlements, were row upon row of pikes.

And impaled upon the point of each pike was a human head.

And, horror upon horror, when I screwed up my eyes and concentrated, I was able to see that each of the human heads was the cranial extremity of an English Test cricketer.

I saw the head of J. W. H. T. "Johnny Won't Hit Today" Douglas.

I saw the heads of A. P. "Tich" Freeman and E. H. "Patsy" Hendren.

I saw E. R. T. Holmes, R. W. V. Robins, A. P. F. Chapman and D. C. S. Compton.

I saw the head of H. D. G. Leveson-Gower.

"I never knew he played for England," I said.

"Neither did I," said Kingsley Kunzel. "I must look it up in Wisden's when we get inside."

He rang the bell of the front door, which was opened instantly by a tiny man with large ears, a prominent hooked nose and hunched and stooping shoulders.

"My God, it's Quasimodo," I said.

"No," said Kingsley Kunzel. "It's Lindsay Hassett."

And with that he took me by the arm and led me up along many corridors and up many flights of stairs until we reached a door of solid teak, which he opened with a key attached to his back collar stud.

He led me inside.

I found myself on a steeply-raked balcony on which were rows of red plush seats.

I looked down below.

And there I saw a large, windowless room with padded walls, dominated by a long strip of coconut matting and two black sightscreens.

"It's the indoor cricket ground," said my chum.

I was about to answer, but he raised his finger.

"Hush," he said. "It's time for their exercise."

And at that came bounding down the pavilion steps three men of truly terrifying appearance.

Their hair was wild.

Their bloodshot eyes rolled most fearfully.

They howled.

They bayed.

They threw themselves on the ground and bit great chunks from the coconut matting.

Yes, it was the Croaker Brothers, the only humans known to natural history to grow a completely new set of teeth each year.

"They're always let out for exercise at this time of day," said Kingsley Kunzel.

I watched them, transfixed with morbid fascination.

So these were the infamous Croaker Brothers.

These were the sons of the terrifying Warren Croaker Senior who had immortalized his name in the annals of the "summer game" when, in a fit of pique, he had beaten to death and eaten an umpire with whose decision he had disagreed.

After weeks of deliberation the Australian Board of Control had decided with typical forthrightness and forcefulness to impose upon him the most stringent punishment on their statute book – a fine of 3s 6d and suspension from all Sheffield Shield Matches for three days, to run concurrently.

The Australian cricketing public was outraged and appalled at the severity of the punishment.

Public demonstrations took place in all the major cities of the Commonwealth.

Petitions were handed in to the Federal Parliament.

Dame Clive James Superstar personally chained itself to the right leg of Mr Edgar Britt during the Melbourne Cup and thus only narrowly missed by the shortest of short heads "a place in the frame".

But it was all fruitless.

The punishment stood.

And so Warren Croaker, forever a man of principle, had decided to turn his back on Australian cricket and retired in voluntary exile to his home in the hills. There he concentrated on inflicting on "the authorities" and the world of cricket his ultimate revenge – his three sons, Warren Junior, Ashley and Sydney-Pete.

He employed the finest tutors in the world for their upbringing – Adolf Hitler, Al Capone, Admiral Dollfuss and Germaine Greer.

He surrounded them with the manifestations of his implacable hatred for the noble, honest, decent and upright cricketers from the Mother Country with their spotless underpants and sweet-smelling socks.

In specially constructed steel-framed display cases were stocked "the booty" of his tours abroad – two half-empty Brylcream bottles said to have been used by Denis Compton, half a dozen meat pies captured during an Old Trafford Test, E. W. Swanton's personal mitre and crozier and scores and scores of similar priceless trophies.

And then came the memorable day when he launched his sons onto the outside cricketing world.

The impact was indeed sensational.

Within three years they had virtually destroyed Test Match cricket as the civilized world had known it.

They and they alone were responsible for the "iconoclast" riots at Headingley when Sir Geoffrey Boycott's priceless rimless spectacles were forever "lost to the nation".

They and they alone provoked the "disgraceful scenes" at Trent Bridge when Dame Peter West's dancing pumps were desecrated at the rear of the commentary box in conditions of indescribable barbarousness.

Fortunately, by an act of extreme valour on the part of Lord Henry Blofeld who single-handedly defended the press box donjon, his patent leather tap shoes were saved for posterity.

I looked on with awed horror as the brothers continued their carnage on the indoor cricket pitch.

I saw Warren Junior rip to shreds with his bare hands the all-weather umpires' toilets.

I saw Ashley devour in a single gulp the three-quarter scale bamboo model of the Grace Gates –

and that without benefit of salt and vinegar.

I saw Sydney-Pete carving with his own hands on the coconut matting pitch the legend: "Kerry Packer Is Innocent OK".

And then . . .

And then down the pavilion steps shuffled an ancient and gossamer-frail figure, clad only in safari boots and MCC touring blanket.

He stopped at a position in the region of deep third man.

He took out from under his blanket a book.

And in a weak little voice he commenced to read.

"Roger, aged seven, and no longer the youngest of the family, ran in wide zigzags, to and fro, across the steep field that sloped up from the lake to Holly Howe, the farm where they were staying for part of their summer holidays."

The effect of this reading was remarkable to behold.

The Croaker brothers ceased their rampaging.

With bent heads they shuffled towards the reader and seated themselves on the ground at his feet.

Over their faces came an expression of benign content.

They listened entranced as the old man continued his reading.

And then all of a sudden it came to me.

I knew that old man!

I had seen him before.

But where?

Where, where, where?

And then I remembered.

I had seen his likeness in a picture of the England touring party of Australia, 1924–25.

He was standing on the back row between M. W. Tate and F. C. Toone (manager).

Of course, of course.

It was . . .

"It's Arthur Dewsbury," I said.

Kingsley Kunzel nodded his head.

"That's right, sport," he said.

And thus did he enravel the mystery that has baffled generations of historians of our beloved "summer game".

As every cricket "buff" knows, it was during the MCC tour of '24 that Arthur Dewsbury disappeared "off the face of the earth".

One minute he was eating hard-baked water biscuits and Vegemite in a Brisbane speak-easy with his England team mates.

Next minute he was gone "ne'er to reappear" on the face of the earth.

Some people claimed he had eloped with Mr W. H. Ponsford.

Others maintained he had succumbed to terminal Nawabs and had been buried at sea to avoid an "international scandal".

"No," said Kingsley Kunzel. "No. He was kidnapped by Warren Senior.

"Arthur bowled him out first ball at Adelaide. Middle stump.

"Well, you know what Warren was like.

"When the umpire's decision went against him, he swore vengeance.

"And so he kidnapped him and threw him into the dungeons here at Croaker Castle."

Sixty years incarceration in Australia!

Sixty years without contact with the civilized world!

Sixty years!

Good God, the poor devil would not have heard of the death of "Stainless" Stephen.

He would be entirely ignorant of the invention of packet soup and wire coat hangers.

"Why, why, why?" I said.

Kingsley Kunzel smiled again.

"He would have let him go," he said. "But then one day he discovered that the only way he could calm his sons was by forcing the old man to read to them.

"He's read the whole canon from 'Bunkle Buts In' to 'We Didn't Mean To Go To Sea.'

"It's the only way to keep them quiet.

"Without him they'd have gone berserk and destroyed the whole world."

Of an instant I was struck by the full horror of the old man's predicament.

I could not help myself.

I leapt to my feet and I shouted at the top of my voice:

"Arthur Dewsbury, Arthur Dewsbury, come home with me.

"Let me take you back to England.

"Come with me now.

"This instant.

"When we return, it will be summer in England."

There was a long silence.

The old man looked up towards where I stood in the balcony.

He strained his rheumy eyes.

He put his hands to his ears.

And then he spoke.

"England in summer?" he said.

"Yes," I said. "Yes, yes, yes."

"But Richie Benaud will be there," he said.

"Yes," I said. "Yes, yes, yes."

He looked at me silently for a moment.

And then he said:

"Bugger off. I'm better off here."

EIGHT

Second Dispatches From The Front

And so we come to Christmas in Melbourne.

Great God! This is an awful place and terrible enough for us to have laboured to find it without the rewards of priority.

Oh, yes it is plain and obvious that others have been here before us.

There are signs all around us of an ancient and primitive culture.

The people are small, stunted and shifty-eyed and look at us with blank and brutish incomprehension when we attempt to trade and barter with them.

Their dwelling places are crude constructions made of empty beer crates and discarded packets of "Fisherman's Friends".

In the centre of the settlement are large stone-built constructions, which, according to archaeological canon, are ancient department stores.

I, however, favour the view that they are elaborate burial mounds, in which the natives buried their dead and accompanying grave goods for the after life – flip-flops, sun tan lotion, zinc ointment, tins of Zubes, family-sized jars of Vegemite and economy-sized cartons of barbecue seasonings.

The natives do attempt to speak a form of pidgin English, but such is the paucity of their vocabulary and the ghastliness of their accent that we British-ers have found it impossible to communicate with them, except by cuffing them soundly round the earhole or by grunting and mumbling in the ursine manner of a Freddie Trueman radio commentary.

When that great traveller, explorer and adven-turer, Lord Henry Blofeld, discovered this region in 1969, he wrote to his brother:

"My dear old thing,

"We have laboured long and hard to find this place.

"The natives of Adelaide had told us many times of the rumours of the existence of a large and primitive society living in conditions of great brutality and odiousness some thousands of miles to the east.

"Well, we have found it, but at what cost to the members of our expedition?

"During the six weeks it took us to attain our objective we lost three portable typewriters, our Arlott patent portable claret dispenser, Matthew Engels of the *Guardian* (I think) and, most tragic of all, a leather bound volume of *Sun* newspaper expense account claim sheets.

"And has it been worth it?

"I believe it has, for little by little I see signs that since our arrival the benevolent forces of the English way of life are beginning to percolate through, albeit slowly, to the natives.

"I am convinced that by the time I return in 1983 it is just possible that the natives will have learned how to tie their own shoelaces and peel back the tops of the cans of weak and tepid beer so beloved in this part of the world."

Alas, his hopes have not been entirely fulfilled.

The huge mounds of empty beer cans in all the public places are evidence that the natives have learned basic can opening skills "of a sort", by using the sharply-filed surfaces of two front teeth.

But the vast numbers of people of both sexes to be seen shuffling round the crude dirt tracks of the settlement with hairy legs, crudely-cut trousers and naked chests seem to suggest that they have not yet learned the talent of doing up their shirt buttons or of performing the skills of elementary depilatory leg waxing.

And so with this background explained to you I present more dispatches for your delectation.

CHRISTMAS DAY

My Christmas message to you all in Blighty is simple – the battle is not lost!

I for one refuse to surrender to the foul, knobbly-kneed, gap-toothed, cheating, belching, swearing, loud-mouthed, hairy-armpitted, chip-shouldered Australians.

I am not a prejudiced man, but I believe with fervour that despite the fact of our having lost two Test Matches, we can still thrash the living daylights out of them.

God is on our side.

So are Roy Plomley and David Jacobs.

With support of that stature we are certain to bring back the Ashes to their rightful resting place.

As long as there is breath left in my plus fours I believe this passionately and unshakeably.

But, my God, it is hard to do so.

Exiled as we are in this godforsaken country of terminal drunks, tram conductors in short trousers and women with big things on the front of their chests it is difficult to remain sanguine.

It is Christmas Day, and my thoughts stray to my friends in dear, dear Witney Scrotum.

Old Grannie Swanton will be hard at work in her dear little cottage kitchen preparing her linseed oil and liniment chutneys for the summer vicarage bring-and-buy sales.

Dotty old Squire Brearley will be poring over his books as he researches for his next masterpiece, "The Cricket of Practical Reason – an Examination of Kantian Theories on 'The Summer Game' in

the Light of the Recent Writings of Soren Kierke-
gaard and Wilfred Wooller".

And in the back yard of the Baxter Arms Don
"Sir Oswald" Mosey will be bayonetting straw
effigies of Miss Monica Sims with his detachment
of junior blackshirts from Keating New Town.

I think of all my friends facing up to another
traditional English Christmas – power cuts, burst
pipes, Julie Andrews and Arthur Scargill's state of
the nation speech from the throne room at Transport House.

And I am filled with wretchedness.

However, the lady wife has tried her damnedest
to make a home-from-home Christmas for Colonel
"Mad" Bob Willis and the troops.

She has rescued them from the fetid bleakness of
their damp and chilly quarters on the banks of the
stinking Yarra River and brought them back to our
quarters.

Here she has chopped up the wardrobe and
bedside table in our squalid, hovel-like hotel
bedroom and, as I write this, an open fire is blazing
merrily in a corner next to the ablutions offices,
and on it she is cooking a traditional Christmas
dinner of boiled pelican in cricket bag sauce.

She has dressed up as Father Christmas and
distributed presents.

For Colonel Bob she has constructed a full-scale
working model of Chris Old, life president (if he

lives that long) of Hypochondriacs Anonymous, and the only fast bowler in the history of the "summer game" ever to have used a runner when opening the bowling for his country.

For Master Pringle she has bought the Alec and Eric Bedser garden gnome colouring book.

As for Derek Randall, she has presented him with a trouser press, and the dear chap is now sitting in it, smiling happily with steam gently hissing out of his earholes.

Yes, I suppose for the moment we are a happy bunch of exiles, despite our incarceration in Melbourne, the hellhole of the southern hemisphere, which more and more reminds me relentlessly of Manchester – only it is colder and rainier and contains far more gormless Northerners with slack jaws and concave shin bones.

And so I raise my glass of home-made corn plaster gin to you all back home and with tears of nostalgia coursing down my cheeks wish you all A Merry Christmas and A Happy New Year.

Oh, to be in England now that Richie Benaud's not there!

THE FIRST DAY

I am not a prejudiced man, but I have to say that watching cricket at the Melbourne Cricket Ground is like sitting in the core of a gigantic suppurating concrete boil.

The overcrowding is intolerable. Once you are inside it is quite impossible to get out, and the security guards and gatemen are offensive in the extreme – in fact, a long-term inmate at Wormwood Scrubs would feel thoroughly at home here.

I blame the lugubrious Innersole, the England team manager, for the miseries inflicted on us this day.

The lady wife and I had decided to forgo the Test Match in favour of a day's indoor wombat-sticking with Alec Bedser.

As we were walking past the vast, brooding, forlorn, inhospitable fastness of the Melbourne Malcolm Hilton hotel we were assailed by Innersole.

He was distraught.

His eyes were wild.

His hair was unkempt.

There were Tizer stains down the front of his lime-green Bermuda shorts.

What was wrong?

He was quick to "blurt it out".

He had heard of the lady wife's proposed defection from the match and thus been faced by open mutiny from Colonel "Mad" Bob Willis and the troops.

If the lady wife did not attend the match, they would not go onto the field of play.

And why?

Because the England team had adopted her as their regimental mascot.

Without her presence, they could not and would not perform.

Innersole pleaded with us.

We must go to the match.

We owed it to Queen and Country and E. W. "Gloria" Swanton.

If the lady wife defected at this crucial time she would ruin forever her chance of appearing on "Desert Island Discs".

At this the lady was persuaded.

Innersole clapped his little pink hands with delight and jumped up and down so violently that he fell out of his surgical sandals.

However, he soon recovered and led us to the ground, where he presented us with tickets and our own personal flares, sonar buoy and anti-exposure suits "in case of emergencies".

Thus began our day of sheer living hell.

Good God, the swines on the gate did everything in their power to keep us out of the ground.

I personally had to queue for three hours, even though I am the holder of the Tony Greig medal for supreme patriotism, which I display prominently in the appropriate place on my hip pocket. Even the worldly, debonair, sophisticated Lord Henry Blofeld had to rattle his sabre most fearsomely before he was let in, disguised as Mrs Bill Frindall.

The lady wife, of course, set about her with shooting stick and golfer's umbrella and soon cleaved a way through the crowds for herself and Colonel Bob and his cohorts.

Conditions were even worse once we had established ourselves inside the ground.

The smell of half-chewed meat pies and semi-regurgitated Bounty Bars was overpowering.

Ragged urchins with adenoids, ricket-crooped legs and transparent big ears clambered like rats over the seats and benches, screaming shrilly and showering us with potato crisp crumbs.

We were not even allowed the consolation of watching the cricket, for the whole ground is designed for the viewing of one thing and one thing alone – the vast electronic scoreboard.

What a verminous contraption.

How typically vulgar.

Its purpose is ostensibly to provide spectators with facts and figures relating to the cricket match taking place at the time – usually in some obscure corner of the ground next to the gents' urinals.

What it does instead is to send out streams of indecipherable Donald Duck films and screen endless repeats of Michael Parkinson chat shows.

Naturally, like all other horrors of the modern world, it was invented by the Japanese.

I had the great good fortune to be taken inside

the monster by Lord Henry Blofeld, whose typewriter wallah had "some pull".

What an amazing sight I beheld – masses of buttons and lights and valves and dials and pulleys and endless belts and, supplying the power for this machinery, pedalling silently at the chain-powered turbines, were twenty thousand tiny Japanese.

What a triumph for the Micronip revolution.

These miseries apart, however, we did have one minor triumph.

It being Sunday, this intensely religious city of rampant call girls and alcohol-crazed car drivers was "dry".

The lady wife and I had, however, "taken precautions".

I had concealed in the false handle of my cricket bat a goodly stock of home-made corn plaster gin, and the lady wife had hidden four litres of Château Koolgoolie Australian Tonic Wine in the false hems of her thermal underpants.

Thus, while the alcohol-starved Australians bayed and bellowed for drink, we were able to sit back in a mellow haze of bliss and superiority, which is, of course, the mark of all Englishmen who visit this repulsive country.

As for the cricket?

Be patient.

We are "on the way".

THE SECOND DAY

Misery! Agony!

The lady wife has this day discovered the whereabouts of Naunton.

A day's cricket irrevocably ruined as with set square and sextant and moving compass she planned the logistics of our visit to the loathesomeness.

I suggested we journey by balloon.

She gave me one of "her looks".

Oh, wretchedness.

THE THIRD DAY

Well, we are within a whisker of soundly thrashing the Australian scum.

I put it down to one thing – the presence of His Sublime and Overwhelming Excellency Michael Parkinson.

What a morale booster for Colonel "Mad" Bob Willis and the troops.

And what a triumph for me.

Yes, it was I, dear readers, who brought him here to this hellhole of the southern hemisphere.

Speaking to him on the talking telephone, I pleaded with him to put forward by one week his annual state visit to Melbourne.

At first the brute was reluctant.

He was "full of excuses".

He said he had to supervise personally the planning of the impending Royal Tour of Australia by the sublime Princess of Wales and her husband, the booby with the big ears and the bald patch.

He said he "could not get out" of his commitment to giving a course of personal hairdressing lessons to Mr Bob Hawke.

He said his wife, Mary Poppins-Parkinson, insisted he stick to his contract of cleaning the windows of the Sydney Opera House.

Finally I persuaded him to come by guaranteeing that I would effect a personal introduction to his heroes, Richie Benaud and Tony Greig, more widely known to the general public as The Beverley Sisters, Babs, Teddy and Billy Wright.

What ecstacy filled my soul when he spoke those magical words:

"Aye. Well. Mm. All reet then."

I had the lady wife up all night polishing the hub caps of the Parkymobile, in which he made his triumphal tour of the ground this morning.

And when His Supreme and Overpowering Munificence entered the English dressing room there wasn't a dry eye in sight.

Poor Master Pringle was completely overcome and fell into a dead swoon.

"The best moment of the tour so far," said the thoroughly nice Mr Jackman.

Finally His Gracious and Stupendously Terrific Majesty bestowed his blessings on the players, and then he was pleased to sit on his portable TV interviewer's commode as the team gathered round his perfectly-formed feet and sang their celebrated war anthem:

"C'mon, Parky.

"C'mon."

The Australians are thoroughly rattled.

Victory is within sight.

My God, the buttons on my plus fours are positively whirring with excitement.

THE FOURTH DAY

Victory is in sight.

And so is the encounter with Naunton.

The horns of a dilemma have never been so pointed.

THE LAST DAY

Oh, ye of little faith.

You did not believe me, when I said victory was certain.

Admit it, of course you didn't, you unpatriotic vermin.

But I knew all along.

And why?

Because the lady wife stepped in three weeks ago to do what the lugubrious Innersole should have done months and months ago – she took charge of the "babes in the wood".

It was patently obvious that Master Pringle and the chaste and innocent Norman Cowans missed one thing and one thing alone – mother love.

And this the lady wife took it upon herself to provide in ample measure.

Each night she tucked up Master Pringle in his own portable self-righting cot and read him fairy stories and extracts from vintage Teddy Tail annuals.

When he was naughty she slapped his wrists, gave him extra prep and made him write out one hundred times:

"I must run faster round the pitch".

And as for dinky Norman – well, she played "Happy Families" with him by the hour.

"Swap you Mr Taylor, the wicket keeper, for Mr Hemmings, the quality greengrocer and fruiterer," she would say, and Norman would shake his woolly head with pleasure, suck his thumb and forthwith subside into "the land of nod".

And the result?

A famous and noble victory for the Englishmen and "Man of the Match" award for their favourite son, Norman Cowans, a direct descendant of Lord Nelson, the Duke of Wellington, Jane Austen and Dame Peter West.

I confess that this last day's play has left me breathless and drained of energy.

I did not see Geoff "Gertrude" Miller's catch, for in my excitement during the final overs of the match my plus fours caught fire spontaneously, and I was only "put out" when the saintly Tony Greig doused me in liberal quantities of his favourite wildly expensive after-shave lotion, Packer Rabone Pour Homme.

And now for Sydney.

I wonder if there is life there as we know it in Witney Scrotum?

I doubt it.

My God, how I doubt it.

NINE

The Lady Wife
Down Under

There comes a time in the life of every lover of the "summer game" when a man has to sit back and calmly and dispassionately "take stock" of his life to date.

It can be a painful business.

The list of his sins and omissions is bound to be long – as it is in all truthfulness for followers of ladies' netball and supporters of bicycle polo.

It behoves us, therefore, to be prudent and prepare ourselves for the final umpire's verdict in that great long room in the sky.

Such an opportunity "came my way" when I found myself stranded in Melbourne awaiting transference to Sydney, which the lugubrious but classically-educated Innersole described so aptly as: "the archetypal bleeding Scylla and Charybdis cock-up of all time".

I was sitting in the foyer of my hotel, idly passing the time by applying lighted matches to the turn-ups of stray Japanese tourists, when it came to me like the icy dagger of fear and foreboding which strikes a man on first hearing the singing voice of Mary O'Hara.

I was getting old.

My run-up was shortened.

My spinning finger was bent and withered.

Activities in the nether regions of the popping crease had long since ceased.

And what had I done with my life?

Well, I had served my King and Country long and faithfully.

I owned a complete collection of the gramophone records of Ann Ziegler and Webster Booth.

I had once been called upon, during an ENSA concert in Mesopotamia, to ask a question of Leslie Welch, the Memory Man.

I had spent many a happy evening with dear friend "Bruce" Woodcock of The Times cutting out patterns for his crepe-de-chine rumpus suits.

But was that enough?

Could a man face his Maker and present that as a complete list of his life's work and expect therefrom to be given the supreme office of Paradise – baggage master to C. H. Parkin?

Obviously not.

Surely there was "something else" to offer?

And then it came to me.

My partner.

Surely in that sphere I had brought happiness and contentment and fulfilment to a fellow human being?

In any partnership between two members of the human race there was bound to be what the immortal E. R. "Elizabeth Regina" Dexter beautifully and profoundly describes as "ups and downs".

The opportunities for dispute and discord are legion.

Propinquity breeds irritation.

Familiarity breeds contempt.

Small issues are all too often "blown up out of all proportion" in even the most ideal of partnerships.

I am convinced, for example, that Denis Compton and Bill Edrich had their little domestic tiffs from time to time.

I am certain beyond shadow of doubt that Cyril Washbrook and the saintly Winston Place were frequently "not on speaking terms".

And nothing will dissuade me from my belief that "all was not as it seemed" between Lindwall and Miller, and that they were constantly rowing over the latter's refusal to help with the washing-up.

Thus it is between myself and the lady wife.

I admit I have not always been perfect.

There have been times when I have "slipped" taking my Friday evening Exlax.

There have been occasions when I have hidden in dark corners and jumped out and delivered a violent and unprovoked kick to the backsides of her confounded Bedlington terriers.

Worse still, I have to record having been unfaithful in unworthy thoughts and dreams concerning "certain aspects" of Herbert Sutcliffe.

But "on the whole" our partnership has flourished and prospered, and a man would not feel ashamed offering this to His Maker as "something to be proud of".

These thoughts consumed me as I left the foyer of the hotel and repaired to the bar, where I ordered a beetroot-based Ring and Toshak tawny port.

Yes, there was no doubt about it, I thought – during the course of our tour Down Under the lady wife and I had "come closer".

Sharing a sleeping compartment on the night Overland Express from Adelaide to Melbourne is bound to involve a certain amount of bodily contact, for climbing into the top bunk necessitates a degree of physical dexterity which would tax a fully-qualified contortionist or a practising member of the Royal Marine Commandos.

We had "come close" too during our stay in Adelaide, when, after having been most fearfully bitten by mosquitos, we had a most cordial mutual de-lousing session in the ablutions offices.

And thus I had come to look at her "in a new light".

There were still, of course, the same old familiar odious features – the piggy little eyes, the eagline nose, the sharp kneecaps, the hectoring voice and the fallen arches.

But there were other things about her, profound aspects of character and behaviour, which, despite our long partnership, I had not noticed.

For example, I had not fully appreciated, until we sat together in the pavilion at the exquisite Adelaide Oval, the loudness of her hand clap.

I can say in all honesty that sitting next to the lady wife whilst she is "in full flood" of applauding is for all the world like sitting in the middle of an Ack Ack battery during the blitz on Liverpool.

I will not deny that it has its advantages.

Without protection of cotton wool plugs no human ear can withstand that volume of noise for long, and thus we soon found ourselves sitting in the middle of a large empty space, which gave us blessed relief from enforced intimacy with the hoggish, pock-marked native Australian vermin.

I am assured, too, by Lord Henry Blofeld, that during the course of one of the lady wife's bouts of applause she completely drowned six and a half minutes of Trevor Bailey's comments on the BBC ball-by-ball commentary.

"My dear old thing," said Lord Henry, "they've awarded Nobel prizes for far less than that."

That apart, what surprised me most of all about the lady wife was her sociability.

I had always regarded her as a person innately hostile to every single member of the human race.

As a frightener of postmen she had no peer.

She was matchless in her inhospitality to my "nearest and dearest" and chums of long standing.

She was supreme in the browbeating of ticket collectors and the intimidation of doorstep Jehovah's Witnesses.

And yet here Down Under she was actually showing signs of benevolence to her fellow men.

She was positively worshipped by members of the travelling English press corps.

The BBC moving television correspondent, Michael Blaikie, came to her room every evening without fail for elocution lessons.

Dear old "Bruce" Woodcock spent hours "on end" at the swimming pool, painting her toenails carmine and fanning her navel with his elbows.

And as for the two representatives from the *Sun* newspaper – they were totally transfixed by her.

Like all their colleagues on that august and revered newspaper they were basically shy and retiring persons.

They just could not cope with the hurly burly of the tour – knowing when to change their pyjamas, wondering which knife to eat their peas from.

And so the lady wife "took them in hand".

She had Lord Henry Blofeld's typewriter wallah instruct them in the mysteries of their portable Olivettis.

Patiently she explained to them the intricacies of

the LBW laws and the umpires' signal system.

She even "helped them out" by giving them exclusive stories, for which the poor wretches slavered in gratitude.

And thus readers of the *Sun* newspaper back home in Blighty were given the first news that Ian Botham had dyed his pubic hairs shocking pink and Dennis Lillee had secretly flown to Mustique to give Princess Margaret a private net during the Melbourne Test.

But it did not end there.

The England cricketers adored her.

Every evening the lugubrious Innersole entertained her in his private suite with toasted tea cakes and grilled pikelets he had flown in daily in the MCC diplomatic bag.

She was privy to the most secret of Colonel "Mad" Bob Willis's battle plans.

Thus she was the first to know of England's secret weapon for Melbourne – they would actually catch the cricket balls propelled in their direction by the Australian batsmen.

Everywhere she went Master Pringle dogged her footsteps, and was awarded from time to time with a bag of dolly mixtures or a packet of liquorice boot laces.

But most amazing of all was her relationship with the wives and sweethearts of the players and journalists.

As all of them have not the slightest interest in, or knowledge of, our beloved "summer game" she dedicated herself to filling in their lonely, lovelorn hours while their menfolk toiled selflessly under blazing sun or in blistering press box bar.

She organized spelling bees, flower arranging classes, works visits, keep-fit sessions, amateur dramatics and foundation garment parties, at one of which Mrs Botham bought a pair of reinforced non-stick underpants for her husband.

But undoubtedly what they appreciated most were the bring-and-buy parties the lady wife held once a week, when the ladies would gather in the bedroom of our hotel, selling their home-embroidered wicket covers and their angora wool typewriter cosies and gossiping softly as they listened to those exquisitely delicate and tasteful programmes on the Australian talking wireless.

How can I describe the voice and accent of the presenter of these programmes?

Imagine a corncrake suffering agonies from early morning piles and screaming out its discomfort.

Think of the sound of a hover mower entangled in a barbed wire fence.

Imagine the noise of a rusty chainsaw cutting through a one ton block of mozzarella cheese.

Put all three together and you have some idea of the quality and sound of that voice.

And it spake thus over the ether:

"Well, it's been another week of high activity here in Melbourne, folks.

"We've had twenty-seven fatal road accidents on the roads, eighteen cases of rape, five of arson and domestic accidents in the home and an outbreak of nude jogging in South Yarra.

"As usual the microphones of station 2XZ566LO have been out and about recording these incidents, and we're pleased to present you with a selection of some of the best.

"I recorded the first one on the microphones of station 2XZ566LO last Tuesday.

"And here it is:

"Well, I'm here standing at the Gobbagobba highway intersection and, geez, there's a car lying completely overturned with its roof ripped off and its four wheels strewn all over the highway and, geez, I can see three people trapped inside.

"Okay, I'm pushing the ambulance people aside and kicking away the resuscitation equipment and I'm trying to talk to one of the passengers and, geez, he's got blood pouring from a gaping wound in his head, and he appears to have very severe bruises and lesions on his neck, and there's a rather jagged-looking shin bone sticking out of the left leg of his trousers.

" 'How are you feeling, pal?

" 'Is that body under the back seat your wife or your girl friend or . . .'

"Oh, geez, he's been sick.

"Well, by looking at the consistency of the aforementioned disgorgement I would guess that shortly before and prior to this bout of nausea he must have consumed a large portion of spaghetti vognole, two chocolate eclairs and five glasses of Valpolicella.

"Well, folks that was last Tuesday, and the score thus far from that road accident on the road is two fatalities and a major amputation.

"We'll keep you posted with the progress.

"And now to an incident, two days later.

"Here goes:

"Well, folks, it's early Thursday morning, and the microphones of station 2XZ566LO are in a house on St Kilda Road, South Yarra, where there's been a rather nasty domestic accident in the home.

"I'm talking to the victim, who seems to be a man in his late fifties.

" 'Excuse me, sir, but do you happen to be a man in your late fifties?'

" 'Yiss.'

" 'And what is the nature of the injury which you have sustained?'

" 'I cut my finger opening a can of tinned fruit.'

" 'Geez! You cut your finger?'

" 'Yiss.'

" 'And did you cut your finger bad?'

" 'No.'

"'Are you absolutely sure and certain regarding that statement?'

"'Yiss.'

"'Am I right, therefore, in assuming that there is no danger of amputation?'

"'Yiss.'

"'And can you tell the listeners of station 2XZ566LO what was the nature of the fruit contained in the can on which you sustained your digital injury?'

"'Peaches.'

"'Geez! Peaches?'

"'Yiss.'

"'Are you certain it wasn't grapefruit segments?'

"'Yiss.'"

What joy, dear readers.

The spirit of Franklin Engelmann and Alvar Liddell lives on.

I finished off my glass of Redpath's temperance eucalyptus rum and with feelings of high good humour flooding through my veins ascended the stairs to our bedroom.

As chance would have it, it was the end of the lady wife's Bring-and-Buy sale, and I smiled benevolently at the ladies as they bade their farewells.

"Cheery bye, Mrs Marlar," I said. "Bought another packet of home-made earache tablets for Gustav, I see."

"Yes," said that lovely lady.

"Toodle-pip, Mrs Willis," I said. "Make sure Colonel Bob takes his Bob Martins tonight, won't you?"

"Yes," said that delightful creature.

I was about to greet the gorgeous Lady Diana Frith when I was grabbed by the scruff of the neck and "hauled inside" the bedroom by the lady wife.

"You!" she said in those familiar bullying cadences. "Where the devil do you think you've been?"

I opened my mouth but no words came.

And I swear at that moment I heard the following words flooding in torrents over my eardrums:

"Well, the microphones of station 2XZ566LO are here in bedroom 467 of the Benaud Regency International Tourist hotel and we are witnessing what promises to be a domestic incident of high drama and . . .

"And, geez, a lady with piggy little eyes, eagline nose and sharp kneecaps is raising her shooting stick and her golfer's umbrella and advancing on . . ."

Bugger it.

Why should I bother?

Let my Maker and E. W. 'Gloria' Swanton sort out my after life.

TEN

A Visit
To Naunton

As I had suspected from the moment we set foot in this desolate, fly-ridden, catarrh-stricken country, when the time came for us to visit the lady wife's unmarried spinster brother, Naunton, she would – to use the parlance of our beloved "summer game" – be "laid low".

The only issue in doubt was as to the nature of the complaint with which she would be afflicted.

Would it be Woolsorter's goitre, Tasmanian milk leg, Hogg cholera, Randall's staggers or the dreaded and incurable Pringle's lethargy?

But no, it was the "old faithful", the galloping Nawabs again, almost certainly the result of exposure to an infected Lamington at a party to commemorate Field Marshal Douglas Jardine's triumphant expedition to Australia in 1932, when the rebellious natives were subdued, routed and finally humiliated during the great Wars of the Bodyline.

Fortunately, in a gesture of typical generosity and overwhelming decency, His Serene and Fully

Harmonious Bounteousness Michael Parkinson "stepped into the breach" and placed at her disposal his own personal flying ambulance, "The Spirit of Angela Rippon", to transport her to Sydney.

This remarkable machine is normally used as winter quarters by Mr Chris Old, but thankfully on this occasion he was away on his annual 100-over service.

We were welcomed on board by the England party's official nanny, Mary Poppins-Parkinson, and, after strapping the lady wife into her own personal luggage rack, I was conducted on a tour of inspection by His Incredible Sumptuousness himself.

With what pride he showed me round the main therapy clinic, with its rows and rows of autocue machines, portable wrinkle removers and microwave toupee restorers.

In the ultra-modern surgical theatre he pointed out the table on which, during an unprecedented seventeen-hour operation, he had witnessed three of the world's top surgeons performing the incredible feat of removing Mr Tony Greig's money belt from his person without use of anaesthetic.

He led me into the newly-installed plastic surgery unit and demonstrated on his own exquisite person the Pat Phoenix patent face-lifter, which he informed me he uses three times daily after meals.

Sadly there was no time to inspect the maternity

ward, where during a flight from Clayton-le-Moors to Taunton Archbishop Fred Rumsey gave birth to Mr Harry Pilling.

And so I bade the lady wife farewell, promising most faithfully that I would use all "my best endeavours" to seek out her loathesome hunk of consanguinity, Naunton, and "pass on her best".

I was conducted to the door of the mobile flying machine by Nanny Poppins-Parkinson, who took me by the arm, kissed me softly on the lips and said in those familiar sweetly-refined tones, which so wondrously grace the world's moving television screens:

"Don't worry theesen, sunshine. Ah'll see t'owd boiler's all reet."

I stood in the airport lounge and watched the plane take off into the vile, cloudless, azure blue sky.

His Fantastic Fulsomeness's personal standard fluttered gaily above the cockpit as he curved the plane low over the runway and did three loop-the-loops and an Immelmann victory roll.

"What an appalling stinker," said Lord Henry Blofeld. "My God, how I hate the nouveau riche."

I shrugged my shoulders and turned away from him.

Such was the refinement of his sensibilities and the purity of his tenderness towards his fellow men he spotted at once that I was in some distress.

"I say, old thing," he said. "Anything wrong?"

In the depths of my misery I could do nothing else but open up my heart and "spill the beans".

Lord Henry's aristocratic lavender blue eyes filled with unrestrained emotion as I recounted my story.

His chief eunuch and monocle wallah applied sweetly-scented hot towels to his cheeks to staunch the flow of tears.

Handkerchiefs of purest Macclesfield silk were pressed delicately to the nostrils of his straight and noble nose by his faithful court jester, the obsequious Keating.

And then he smiled.

What a radiant sight.

What music to my ears as he spoke thus:

"My dear old thing, do admit. I cannot bear to see a chum in such distress. Pray allow me to place myself at your disposal.

"I shall myself conduct you to the vile wilderness of the Outback to visit your detestable brother-in-law.

"We shall travel by my personal train."

And thus did I find myself the following morning standing in the concourse of Melbourne's Flinders Street station as Lord Henry arrived in the state open landau to prepare for his departure.

What a magnificent sight it all made.

The bejewelled and turbaned Sikh warriors of Lord Henry's personal bodyguards stood rigidly to attention at one-yard intervals along the platform.

The crowd surged forward in a heaving, steaming, stinking mass in an attempt to catch a sight of Lord Henry.

But already he was far from their miserable, narrow-gutted gaze, standing at the head of his personal train, tossing egg and cress sandwiches to the engine driver.

He greeted me warmly.

"My dear old thing," he said. "What a perfectly topping day. Do admit."

He smiled once more and pointed to the cerise-and-ochre-painted locomotive that stood at his side, flanks heaving, boiler rumbling, valves snarling, exhaust snorting.

"Not bad, eh?" he said.

"It's an A2 class 4–6–0 with Walschaerts valve gear and O.S. Nock side-link, double-coupled pressurized smoke deflectors.

"I got it for a song from 'a little man' in North Williamstown."

He grasped my arm and, leading me along the platform to his personal quarters, proudly pointed out to me some of the fascinating carriages which made up his train.

There was an old LMS indoor cricket car with clerestory roof and bogie sightscreens.

There were the three armoured mobile barracks and stables for Lord Henry's Ghurka infantrymen and his Prussian cavalry.

There was an old LNER concubines' sleeping car.

And there was the extremely rare MCC Railways six-wheel corridor pavilion with heavy roller and detachable scoreboard.

At length we came to his personal quarters and stepped inside.

What magnificence.

What elegance.

What contrast to the vulgar cheapness of Parkinson's personal quarters in his flying ambulance.

There the cork-tiled walls were lined with glossy, autographed photographs of second-rate, conceited, talentless performers from the moving television and kinematograph screen, dominated by the full length Annigoni portrait of Dame Kerry Ann Wright inscribed "To Mike with Admiration. Always. Kerry and Buzz".

In Lord Henry's quarters, on the other hand, the walls were lined with exquisite tapestries, priceless velvet drapes and paintings he had personally commissioned by the world's leading artists.

I particularly admired his Hockney, "Ken Higgs and Fred Swarbrook, Poolside, Trentham Gardens".

And I positively purred with pleasure at his superb Sydney Nolan, "Norm O'Neill, K. D. 'Slasher' MacKay, Ron Saggers and the Eureka Stockade Affair".

How reassuring, I thought, to find such sophistication and unrestrained opulence flourishing amidst the base vulgarity and mediocrity of the modern world.

"But this, my dear old thing, is my proudest possession," said Lord Henry, and he held up a green flag.

I shook my head with puzzlement.

His gay laughter tinkled among the rims of the Bohemian crystal bail holders and the Waterford glass umpires' tokens.

"It's a guard's flag," he said. "It belonged to Ted Dexter's dad."

And with that he hopped out of his carriage, raised his flag, and the train slowly pulled out of the platform, to the accompaniment of the deafening cheers of the crowds and the sweet melody of a Chopin nocturne played in the GWR piano coach by The Master of Lord Henry's Musick, Dame André Previn.

We dined that night on exotic foods specially prepared by chefs recruited from the world's finest establishments of haute cuisine, and I confess I felt an inward sneer of contempt as I thought of that brute Parkinson, who would at that moment, I knew, be sitting in his shirt tails and braces stuffing his repulsive face with Moreton Bay bugs on toast and Barnsley bus station bread cakes.

We drank vintage wines from France and the Palatinate.

We listened to madrigals sung by his personal choir of castrati.

We watched the antics of the court jester, the obsequious Keating, as he did his celebrated act of balancing one-legged on the edge of a Guardian expense account sheet and juggled simultaneously three jars of caviare, a tin of Beluga dubbin and a phial of Doctor Compton's hangover tablets.

And, of course, we talked on and on and on into the deepest fastnesses of the night.

It was then and during our subsequent three days' journey that I "got to know" Lord Henry.

As the train continued its stately progress through the remotest parts of the wild and savage and barren Australian outback Lord Henry insisted on stopping at the rudest and most isolated of wayside halts, where he would present himself to the wondering, grovelling, simple sheep-shearers and their ragged families and toss them gifts of game pâté, raspberry-flavoured pastillines and patent leather polo boots.

Such generosity of spirit.

Such purity of emotion.

However, to me the most revealing moment came as we were sitting in the Great Northern Railway gentlemen's sauna and massage parlour, where Lord Henry was having his eyebrows plucked by sensuous, sinuous young maidens dressed in nothing but the uniform of ticket collectors of the Cheshire

Lines Railway.

He turned to me quite suddenly and said "out of the blue":

"My dear old thing, you know what's wrong with the current England team, don't you?

"It's not that they can't play cricket.

"It's just that they're so frightfully common.

"Do admit."

It was an hour later that we reached our destination, Koolgoolie Creek.

How can I do "full justice" to a description of the wretchedness of that township?

Over all hung the smell of stale chips and untreated athlete's foot.

The corrugated iron roofs of the mean public buildings sagged, hag-backed and brow-beaten.

Bare-footed, unshaven, matted-haired men sat on their haunches in the arid red dust.

"Just like the Saturday of the Oval Test," said Lord Henry.

He paused and stared at me intently.

"I'm afraid it's up to you now, old thing," he said.

I nodded.

"I shall await your return here," he said.

"For your safety I shall place at your disposal my personal subahdar, the Raikbar Kapil Dev and a detachment of The Independent Bengali Leg Tweakers.

"But from this moment on it is you and you alone."

He shook me warmly by the hand, and thus did I begin my quest for Naunton.

The township was even more wretched than I had first seen from the train.

It consisted of a narrow main street made up of seventeen grog shops, three public houses, seven doss houses, one metholated spirits distillery and a clinic for sick camels and distressed drunks.

A collection of adobe huts clustered round a dried-out, fly-crazed pond housed the inhabitants, and it was to one of these I was directed by a half-caste abo with flat nose, bloodshot eyes and grey-stubbled chin, who bore a marked resemblance to Mr Warren Mitchell.

The hut was slightly larger than its fellows.

Outside it stood a crooked notice board on which was printed:

"Anglo-Koolgoolie Import and Export Trading Pty.

"Prop. Naunton . . ."

Here there were several surnames, each of which had been erased by liberal applications of dried wallaby dung.

I knocked on the front door.

It fell down instantly.

I felt a momentary shaft of fear, but the presence of the massive Kapil Dev and the grinning Bengali Leg Tweakers reassured me, and I stepped inside.

There was an overpowering smell of Thermogene, but in the stygian gloom I could make out none of the features of the single room which formed the entire ground floor of the building.

Holding tight to Kapil Dev's shirt tail I stumbled towards the patch of light which emanated from a gap in the planking of the back door.

I groped at it with my hand.

The door fell down instantly.

And there revealed to us was a dusty, oil-streaked back yard.

It was littered with a mass of rusting metal implements.

There were splintered pick-axes, dented zinc baths and a rickety wooden structure, which to my untutored eye looked remarkably like a pit head winding gear I had once seen at the Lowson Deep Colliery, Wardle Common.

And, bending over a shallow pit at the far end of the yard, shaking a large wooden sieve, was a figure which even at that distance I recognized instantly as the lady wife's loathesome, unmarried spinster brother, Naunton.

"Naunton!" I shouted.

The figure turned, and I saw at once that it was indeed he.

He was wearing nothing but bush hat and lady's purple cami-knickers, although I am bound to say he was wearing "passable" make-up.

When he saw me, he fell to the ground and

commenced to gibber in the most frenzied manner.

"You've not brought Hitler, have you?" he said, clutching at the leg of my plus fours.

"Tell me you've not brought Ghengis Khan or Attila the Hun."

"No, Naunton," I said. "The lady wife is indisposed."

The look of relief on his face was pitiful to behold.

His false eyelashes fluttered with emotion and the mascara ran in rivulets down his rouged cheeks.

I looked at him silently for a moment and then I pointed at the wooden sieve and said:

"What the devil are you doing with that?"

"Panning for cricket balls," he replied.

"What?"

"This used to be the finest cricket ball mine in the whole of Australia," he said.

"Since I've been here all I've brought up are three golf balls and half a badminton shuttlecock.

"Typical of my luck."

And with that he burst into tears and rolled over onto his back, kicking his front legs in the air.

It took me the best part of an hour and a half to "calm him" but then, after consuming a "goodly" portion of my flask of home-made corn plaster gin, he recovered sufficiently to take me into the downstairs room of his hovel and in a weak, cracked voice tell me something of the history of his long exile in this odious land of Greek taxi drivers and

Wop brothel-keepers.

His story was typical of the millions of misguided immigrants from the Mother Country who set sail for this so-called "land of milk and honey" imagining they would earn "fame and fortune".

He had set himself up as Australia's first flying piano tuner.

Failure.

He had bought the exclusive franchise for the marketing of thermal spats.

Failure.

He had acquired the sole Australian rights for Colonel Swanton's Kentucky Fried Welsh Rarebit.

Failure.

Disaster had followed disaster.

"But why, Naunton?" I asked. "Why?"

He took another "slug" of my corn plaster gin, adjusted the beauty spot on his right thigh and said with heavy voice:

"It was the Thermogene that did it."

"Thermogene?" I said. "Thermogene?"

"Yes," he said. "I became an addict of Thermogene sniffing."

And so he revealed the full horror of his predicament.

Incarcerated in the bleak outback of Australia, deprived of the consolation of the cricket commentaries of Richie Benaud and the writings of Dame

Clive James Superstar, he had turned, like so many others before, to the comfort of Thermogene sniffing.

And thus had he fallen prey to the clutches of the Melbourne Mafia and been forced into the role of pusher.

It had been his ruination.

From Thermogene he "had graduated" to the hard stuff – Vick cough drops, menthol millet sprays and California syrup of figs.

Inevitably he had been apprehended by the authorities, and, but for the intervention of "people in high places", would have found himself punished most direly with the ultimate deterrent known to Australian jurisprudence – two days' solitary confinement with Ian Chappell.

He had been "let off lightly".

He had been banished to Koolgoolie Creek on the understanding that never again would he "show his face" in civilized society.

I looked at him with pity.

"You poor devil," I said. "Still, at least you'll never ever in the whole of your life have to see a Michael Parkinson chat show again."

He smiled weakly.

"Yes," he said. "That is a great consolation."

And then of a sudden he threw himself to his knees and clawed at my plus fours once more.

"There's only one thing kept me going through all

these trials and tribulations," he sobbed. "Do you know what it is? Do you? Do you? Do you?"

I cuffed him soundly round the back of the neck with my stumper's mallet and said:

"No, what is it?"

And with that he "positively" screamed at the top of his voice:

"The thought that I'd never ever ever in the whole of my life see my sister again.

"And now you've turned up.

"You're going to bring her here, aren't you? Aren't you? Aren't you?"

He hurled himself on his back again and wailed.

"What am I to do?"

I looked down on him, and I confess that feelings of the deepest concern and sympathy flooded through my soul.

I thought for a moment, and then I had "a sudden shaft" of inspiration.

From my hip pocket I took out the airmail envelope in which I had intended to insert the latest of my dispatches to the Commodore.

"This is what we'll do," I said.

And with that I took hold of his head and into the envelope shook the vast mass of dandruff which infested his tangled, scrofulous hair.

"I'll give this to the lady wife," I said.

"I shall say that you are dead, and that these are your ashes."

My God, how the brute howled with gratitude and relief.

He smothered my cheeks with kisses.

He pounded me on the back, shook his earrings like a dervish and twanged the elastic in his knickers like Julian Bream playing a Spanish fandango.

And then he fell into a dead swoon.

I left him there and then.

There was nothing more I could do.

I returned to Lord Henry's train.

We journeyed to Sydney and there I presented the envelope to the lady wife and told her "my story".

She looked at the envelope silently for a moment.

Then she opened it, sniffed its contents, looked at it once more and said:

"Typical of him. He hasn't even bothered to put a stamp on it."

ELEVEN

Third Dispatches From The Front

THE ARRIVAL IN SYDNEY

We marched into Sydney this day heads high, jaws strutting, spirits soaring – yes, we had beaten the Australian scum at Melbourne.

And what a welcome the crowds gave us.

And why not?

At long last we had beaten the loathesome Greg Chappell and his gum-chewing, hip-slinking, foul-coiffeured brigands and brought his army of occupation to an end.

Once again sportsmanship was the victor.

Once again England was in the ascendancy.

Fair play was rampant and liberated, and those delightful folk "on the Hill" could once more express their essential natures – gentle, fair-minded, sensitive, delicate-mouthed and dedicated to the cause of orphaned cockatoos and distressed Rodney Marshes.

You see, for far too long the sublimely innocent

Australian cricketing public has had to bow its head beneath the tyranny of aluminium bats, underarm lobs and the cruellest dictatorship known to modern twentieth century history – the Chappell brothers' Junta.

No wonder the people of Sydney cheered us to the echo as we marched through the streets, bats rampant, thigh pads swinging and the harnesses of our jock straps jangling gaily in the ghastly Antarctic gales.

What a magnificent sight Colonel "Mad" Bob Willis and his troops made.

There was our leader mounted in the van of the parade on the huge, barrel-chested drum horse, Botham.

Behind came the dashing Lt. the Hon David Gower of the 4th Leicester Lancers, struggling to keep in check his rippling, prancing battle charger, Cowans.

And, yes, there was peppery Major Jackman cuffing into step the loyal foot soldiers Private Hemmings, Bombardier Fowler, dear old ragged Sapper Randall with the massed earrings of Cornet Pringle glinting in the sunlight.

How my heart surged with pride.

And then, as the English troops swung through the portals of the Sydney Cricket Ground, sheer ecstacy.

For there, standing on the saluting base, was none other than Lady Falklander in person.

With typical patriotic self-sacrifice she had flown over especially to "take the salute".

How ringing was her voice as she addressed the men:

"You have scored a great and glorious victory," she said.

"You have shown the free world that tyranny and oppression will never be tolerated in a society in which I myself and Sir Geoffrey Boycott hold sway.

"With pride and emotion I saw you in action at Melbourne.

"I saw every second of your batting.

"I counted you all in.

"I counted you all out.

"And now I say to each and every one of you —

"Rejoice, gentlemen.

"Rejoice."

And then it rained.

It rained! Eleven thousand miles from Manchester and it rained!

Is there no end to the hideousnesses this godforsaken country inflicts on us?

Is there really blessed death after a commentary by Richie Benaud?

THE REST DAY

We spent our rest day most agreeably.

In the company of the lugubrious Innersole, team manager of the England tourists, and their chaperon Nanny Mary Poppins-Parkinson, we visited one of Australia's most revered historical monuments – the Château Benaud.

Here was born Richie, first, second and third Duke of Benaud, known to all the world as "the Queen Mother of Australian cricket" – although I myself personally do not think he has aged half so well as that lovely and gracious lady.

However, despite all the evidence to the contrary from his appearances on the moving television screen, the "old boy" is alive and well and in full possession of his faculties.

Indeed he greeted us in a mood of some elation, having just learned he had been appointed chief fashion consultant to Jim Laker (trousers division). Nothing was too much trouble for him.

He personally led us to the dank cave wherein lives the Blessed Tony Greig of the Sorrows, dedicated to a life of total penury and prayer for one-parent county cricketers and short-sighted Australian umpires – who have been much in evidence during this series.

He also introduced us to that celebrated scholar and President of the Royal Society for Dropped

Aitches, Professor F. S. Trueman.

The great man is currently touring this detestable country, delivering his lecture: "How I personally in person and on my own won single-handedly games too numerous to mention for England, saved Test Match cricket as we know it for posterity and even farther and thus became Brian Close Emeritus Professor of Difficult Sums at Cambridge University".

On leaving his residence the Duke presented the lady wife with an autographed, unused set of Greg Chappell's teeth and yours truly with an autographed copy of his latest book, "The Wit of Richie Benaud", which I unfortunately lost a short time later through a small hole in the hip pocket of my plus fours.

On the way home Innersole was moved to tears.

"Do you know," he said to the lady wife. "I firmly believe that Test Match cricket would be so much better if it consisted entirely of rest days."

So say I.

In my opinion it is the only way to keep off our moving television screens in Blighty the vile Benaud.

When I return to the Mother Country I intend to form a society to compel the loathesomeness to spend six months quarantine twice a year before he is allowed to enter our country.

THE FINAL DAY

Well, we lost.

I do not blame Colonel "Mad" Bob Willis and his troops.

I do not blame the England manager, the lugubrious Innersole, even though he has "taken a shine" to the lady wife and showered her with endless gifts of pipe cleaners, bulldog clips, Swedish smoking tobacco and Danish musical tuning forks.

No, I blame one thing and one thing alone – the overwhelming hideousness of Australia.

It is asking the impossible of a civilized and cultured country such as dear old Albion to play the world's most noble game in a land of sex-craved turnstile attendants, hairy-eared bus drivers and ablutions offices designed more for kangaroos than upright, upstanding, blue-blooded Britons.

I am not a prejudiced man, but this country does "strange things" to a man.

Consider the case of Alec Bedser.

Only yesterday I caught him at the back of the pavilion skate-boarding, dressed only in maroon socks and grey plastic raincoat.

And then half an hour later I had occasion to severely reprimand Brian Johnston and Mrs Gustav Marlar who were playing frisbee with Frank Tyson's spare portable toupee.

It is the heat, you see.

We return, the lady wife and I, to Witney Scrotum with pride and with defiance.

And in the false bottom of my cricket bag I carry the Ashes.

Yes, dear readers, they are not lost.

On display for the next five years in the long room at Lords will be placed the Ashes of the foullest thing we have encountered during our tour of this disgusting and obscene country – the exit visa which allowed Olive Newton St John to inflict her horrendousness on the civilized world as we know and love it.

Victory is ours.

Right has triumphed.

TWELVE

The Return

It is spring in Witney Scrotum.

Snow shrouds the summit of Botham's Gut.

Sheets of hail sweep over the water meadows at Cowdrey's Bottom.

The house martins have returned to the eaves of the Commodore's summer house.

The chiff-chaffs have returned to the copse at the rear of the Baxter Arms.

The acne has returned to the neck of dear Miss Roebuck in the dog biscuit shop.

And the lady wife and I have returned to the domestic hearth.

The log fire roars in the inglenook grate.

The wind sighs and soughs through the rafters of the cock loft.

We switch on the moving television screen.

And there!

And there!

"And now over to Sydney to give his summing up of play on the seventeenth day of the Royal Tour here is Richie Benaud."

I am not a prejudiced man, but . . .